I0759689

Church Pocket Book and Diary 2026

with Lectionary

Personal memoranda

Name ....

Address (home) ....

....

....

Telephone ....

Mobile ....

Email ....

Address (work) ....

....

....

Telephone ....

Email ....

Blood group ....

In case of emergency please notify: ....

Name ....

Address ....

....

....

Telephone ....

Mobile ....

Email ....

Church Pocket Book and Diary 2026
ISBN 978-0-281-09108-9 (Sunflowers)
ISBN 978-0-281-09109-6 (Black)

Printed in Turkey by Mega Basim

Contents

Calendar 2026

JANUARY						
Su	.	X^2	B	E^2	E^3	..
M	.	5	12	19	26	..
Tu	.	E	13	20	27	..
W	.	7	14	21	28	..
Th	1	8	15	22	29	..
F	2	9	16	23	30	..
Sa	3	10	17	24	31	..

FEBRUARY						
Su	E^4	L^{-2}	L^{-1}	L^1	..	..
M	Pr	9	16	23	..	..
Tu	3	10	17	24	..	..
W	4	11	A	25	..	..
Th	5	12	19	26	..	..
F	6	13	20	27	..	..
Sa	7	14	21	28	..	..

MARCH						
Su	L^2	L^3	L^4	L^5	P	..
M	2	9	16	23	30	..
Tu	3	10	17	24	31	..
W	4	11	18	An	..	..
Th	5	12	19	26	..	..
F	6	13	20	27	..	..
Sa	7	14	21	28	..	..

APRIL						
Su	.	E	E^2	E^3	E^4	..
M	.	6	13	20	27	..
Tu	.	7	14	21	28	..
W	1	8	15	22	29	..
Th	M	9	16	23	30	..
F	G	10	17	24	..	..
Sa	4	11	18	25	..	..

MAY						
Su	.	E^5	E^6	E^7	W	T
M	.	4	11	18	25	..
Tu	.	5	12	19	26	..
W	.	6	13	20	27	..
Th	.	7	A	21	28	..
F	1	8	15	22	29	..
Sa	2	9	16	23	30	..

JUNE						
Su	.	T^1	T^2	T^3	T^4	..
M	1	8	15	22	29	..
Tu	2	9	16	23	30	..
W	3	10	17	24	..	..
Th	4	11	18	25	..	..
F	5	12	19	26	..	..
Sa	6	13	20	27	..	..

The Calendars for 2026 and 2027 follow *The New Lectionary and Calendar*

Key to calendar notes (continued on pages 5 and 6)

A = Ash Wednesday, Ascension, Advent
A^- = Before Advent
A^{-4} = also All Saints, 2027 (if transferred)
A^{-1} = Christ the King
An = Annunciation
AS = All Saints (also Fourth Sunday before Advent, 2026)

Calendar 2026

JULY						
Su	.	T^{5}	T^{6}	T^{7}	T^{8}	..
M	.	6	13	20	27	..
Tu	.	7	14	21	28	..
W	1	8	15	22	29	..
Th	2	9	16	23	30	..
F	3	10	17	24	31	..
Sa	4	11	18	25	..	..

AUGUST						
Su	.	T^{9}	T^{10}	T^{11}	T^{12}	T^{13}
M	.	3	10	17	24	31
Tu	.	4	11	18	25	..
W	.	5	12	19	26	..
Th	.	6	13	20	27	..
F	.	7	14	21	28	..
Sa	1	8	15	22	29	..

SEPTEMBER						
Su	.	T^{14}	T^{15}	T^{16}	T^{17}	..
M	.	7	14	21	28	..
Tu	1	8	15	22	29	..
W	2	9	16	23	30	..
Th	3	10	17	24	..	..
F	4	11	18	25	..	..
Sa	5	12	19	26	..	..

OCTOBER						
Su	.	T^{18}	T^{19}	T^{20}	T^{L}	..
M	.	5	12	19	26	..
Tu	.	6	13	20	27	..
W	.	7	14	21	28	..
Th	1	8	15	22	29	..
F	2	9	16	23	30	..
Sa	3	10	17	24	31	..

NOVEMBER						
Su	AS	A^{-3}	A^{-2}	A^{-1}	A	..
M	2	9	16	23	30	..
Tu	3	10	17	24	..	..
W	4	11	18	25	..	..
Th	5	12	19	26	..	..
F	6	13	20	27	..	..
Sa	7	14	21	28	..	..

DECEMBER						
Su	..	A^{2}	A^{3}	A^{4}	X^{1}	..
M	..	7	14	21	28	..
Tu	1	8	15	22	29	..
W	2	9	16	23	30	..
Th	3	10	17	24	31	..
F	4	11	18	X	..	..
Sa	5	12	19	26	..	..

B = Baptism
E = Epiphany, Easter
(E^{3} = also Conversion of Paul, 2026)
E^{4} = also Presentation (if transferred)
G = Good Friday
L = Lent
L^{-} = Before Lent
M = Maundy Thursday

Calendar 2027

JANUARY

Su	.	X^2	B	E^2	E^3	E^4
M	.	4	11	18	25	..
Tu	.	5	12	19	26	..
W	.	E	13	20	27	..
Th	.	7	14	21	28	..
F	1	8	15	22	29	..
Sa	2	9	16	23	30	..

FEBRUARY

Su	.	L^{-1}	L^1	L^2	L^3	..
M	1	8	15	22	..	..
Tu	Pr	9	16	23	..	..
W	3	A	17	24	..	..
Th	4	11	18	25	..	..
F	5	12	19	26	..	..
Sa	6	13	20	27	..	..

MARCH

Su	.	L^4	L^5	P	E	..
M	1	8	15	22	29	..
Tu	2	9	16	23	30	..
W	3	10	17	24	31	..
Th	4	11	18	M	..	..
F	5	12	19	G	..	..
Sa	6	13	20	27	..	..

APRIL

Su	.	E^2	E^3	E^4	E^5	..
M	.	An	12	19	26	..
Tu	.	6	13	20	27	..
W	.	7	14	21	28	..
Th	1	8	15	22	29	..
F	2	9	16	23	30	..
Sa	3	10	17	24	..	..

MAY

Su	.	E^6	E^7	W	T	T^1
M	.	3	10	17	24	31
Tu	.	4	11	18	25	..
W	.	5	12	19	26	..
Th	.	A	13	20	27	..
F	.	7	14	21	28	..
Sa	1	8	15	22	29	..

JUNE

Su	.	T^2	T^3	T^4	T^5	..
M	.	7	14	21	28	..
Tu	1	8	15	22	29	..
W	2	9	16	23	30	..
Th	3	10	17	24	..	..
F	4	11	18	25	..	..
Sa	5	12	19	26	..	..

P = Palm Sunday
Pr = Presentation
T = Trinity
(T^9 = also James, 2027)
(T^{12} = also The Blessed Virgin Mary, 2027)
(T^{20} = also Luke, 2026)
T^L = Last Sunday after Trinity
W = Pentecost (Whit Sunday)
X = Christmas
(X^1 = also John, 2026; Stephen, 2027)
X^2 = also Epiphany, 2026 (if transferred)

Calendar 2027

JULY						
Su	.	T^{6}	T^{7}	T^{8}	T^{9}	..
M	.	5	12	19	26	..
Tu	.	6	13	20	27	..
W	.	7	14	21	28	..
Th	1	8	15	22	29	..
F	2	9	16	23	30	..
Sa	3	10	17	24	31	..

AUGUST						
Su	T^{10}	T^{11}	T^{12}	T^{13}	T^{14}	..
M	2	9	16	23	30	..
Tu	3	10	17	24	31	..
W	4	11	18	25	..	..
Th	5	12	19	26	..	..
F	6	13	20	27	..	..
Sa	7	14	21	28	..	..

SEPTEMBER						
Su	.	T^{15}	T^{16}	T^{17}	T^{18}	..
M	.	6	13	20	27	..
Tu	.	7	14	21	28	..
W	1	8	15	22	29	..
Th	2	9	16	23	30	..
F	3	10	17	24	..	..
Sa	4	11	18	25	..	..

OCTOBER						
Su	.	T^{19}	T^{20}	T^{21}	T^{L}	A^{-4}
M	.	4	11	18	25	..
Tu	.	5	12	19	26	..
W	.	6	13	20	27	..
Th	.	7	14	21	28	..
F	1	8	15	22	29	..
Sa	2	9	16	23	30	..

NOVEMBER						
Su	.	A^{-3}	A^{-2}	A^{-1}	A	..
M	AS	8	15	22	29	..
Tu	2	9	16	23	30	..
W	3	10	17	24	..	..
Th	4	11	18	25	..	..
F	5	12	19	26	..	..
Sa	6	13	20	27	..	..

DECEMBER						
Su	..	A^{2}	A^{3}	A^{4}	X^{1}	..
M	..	6	13	20	27	..
Tu	..	7	14	21	28	..
W	1	8	15	22	29	..
Th	2	9	16	23	30	..
F	3	10	17	24	31	..
Sa	4	11	18	X	..	..

MOVEABLE FEASTS 2025–2035

Year	Ash Wednesday		Easter Day		Ascension Day		Pentecost Whit Sunday		First Sunday of Advent		Christmas Day
2025	Mar	5	Apr	20	May	29	June	8	Nov	30	Thu
2026	Feb	18	Apr	5	May	14	May	24	Nov	29	Fri
2027	Feb	10	Mar	28	May	6	May	16	Nov	28	Sat
2028	Mar	1	Apr	16	May	25	June	4	Dec	3	Mon
2029	Feb	14	Apr	1	May	10	May	20	Dec	2	Tue
2030	Mar	6	Apr	21	May	30	June	9	Dec	1	Wed
2031	Feb	26	Apr	13	May	22	June	1	Nov	30	Thu
2032	Feb	11	Mar	28	May	6	May	16	Nov	28	Sat
2033	Mar	2	Apr	17	May	26	June	5	Nov	27	Sun
2034	Feb	22	Apr	9	May	18	May	28	Dec	3	Mon
2035	Feb	7	Mar	25	May	3	May	13	Dec	2	Tue

Notes to the diary pages

In the following diary pages, names of Sundays (in **bold** type) are in accordance with *The Common Worship Calendar and Lectionary*, with the titles preferred by The Book of Common Prayer (in *italic* type) being listed beneath them. Festivals (in **bold** type) are distinguished by *CW* and BCP when the calendars diverge, and when the rules require a Festival to be transferred, the alternative date is shown. Principal Feasts and other Principal Holy Days are in **BOLD CAPITALS**. Other days and traditional titles are in ordinary type. For *The Common Worship Calendar and Lectionary* applied to December 2025 and in full to the year 2026, see the Lectionary on pages 134–280.

Astronomical and Calendarial information is reproduced with permission.

Certain dates are subject to change and regional variation.

30 Sunday **The First Sunday of Advent**
1 in Advent

1 Monday **Andrew the Apostle**
Bank Holiday (Scotland)

2 Tuesday

Wednesday **3**

Thursday **4**

Friday **5**

Saturday **6**

December 2025

7 Sunday **The Second Sunday of Advent**
2 in Advent

8 Monday

9 Tuesday

Ember Day (CW) Wednesday **10**

Thursday **11**

Ember Day (CW) Friday **12**

Ember Day (CW) Saturday **13**

December 2025

14 Sunday **The Third Sunday of Advent**

3 in Advent

15 Monday

16 Tuesday

Ember Day (BCP) Wednesday **17**

Thursday **18**

Ember Day (BCP) Friday **19**

Ember Day (BCP) Saturday **20**

December 2025

21 Sunday **The Fourth Sunday of Advent**
4 in Advent

22 Monday **Thomas the Apostle** (BCP)
(*CW* 3 July)

23 Tuesday

Christmas Eve Wednesday **24**

CHRISTMAS DAY Thursday **25**
Bank Holiday (England, N. Ireland, Scotland, Wales and Rep. of Ireland)

Stephen, Deacon, First Martyr Friday **26**
Bank Holiday (England, N. Ireland, Scotland, Wales and Rep. of Ireland)

John, Apostle and Evangelist Saturday **27**

December 2025

28 Sunday

The First Sunday of Christmas
Sunday after Christmas Day
The Holy Innocents

29 Monday

30 Tuesday

Wednesday **31**

Thursday **1**

The Naming and Circumcision of Jesus (*CW*)
The Circumcision of Christ (BCP)
Bank Holiday (England, N. Ireland, Scotland, Wales and Rep. of Ireland)

Friday **2**

Bank Holiday (Scotland)

Saturday **3**

January 2026

4 Sunday **The Second Sunday of Christmas**
2 after Christmas

5 Monday

6 Tuesday **THE EPIPHANY**

Wednesday **7**

Thursday **8**

Friday **9**

Saturday **10**

January 2026

11 Sunday

The Baptism of Christ
1 after Epiphany

12 Monday

13 Tuesday

Wednesday **14**

Thursday **15**

Friday **16**

Saturday **17**

January 2026

18 Sunday

The Second Sunday of Epiphany
2 after Epiphany
The Week of Prayer for
Christian Unity until 25th

19 Monday

20 Tuesday

Wednesday **21**

Thursday **22**

Friday **23**

Saturday **24**

January 2026

25 Sunday

The Third Sunday of Epiphany
3 after Epiphany
The Conversion of Paul

26 Monday

27 Tuesday

Wednesday **28**

Thursday **29**

Friday **30**

Saturday **31**

February 2026

1 Sunday

The Fourth Sunday of Epiphany

Septuagesima

2 Monday

THE PRESENTATION OF CHRIST IN THE TEMPLE (CANDLEMAS)

3 Tuesday

Wednesday **4**

Thursday **5**

Friday **6**

Saturday **7**

February 2026

8 Sunday **The Second Sunday before Lent**

Sexagesima

9 Monday

10 Tuesday

Wednesday **11**

Thursday **12**

Friday **13**

Saturday **14**

February 2026

15 Sunday

The Sunday next before Lent
Quinquagesima
Thomas Bray, founder of
SPCK (died 1730)

16 Monday

17 Tuesday

ASH WEDNESDAY Wednesday **18**

Thursday **19**

Friday **20**

Saturday **21**

February 2026

22 Sunday **The First Sunday of Lent**
1 in Lent

23 Monday

24 Tuesday **Matthias the Apostle** (BCP)
(CW 14 May)

Ember Day (*CW* and BCP) Wednesday **25**

Thursday **26**

Ember Day (*CW* and BCP) Friday **27**

Ember Day (*CW* and BCP) Saturday **28**

March 2026

1 Sunday

The Second Sunday of Lent

2 in Lent

2 Monday

3 Tuesday

Wednesday **4**

Thursday **5**

Friday **6**

Saturday **7**

8 Sunday **The Third Sunday of Lent**
3 in Lent

9 Monday

10 Tuesday

March 2026

Wednesday **11**

Thursday **12**

Friday **13**

Saturday **14**

March 2026

15 Sunday

The Fourth Sunday of Lent

4 in Lent

Mothering Sunday

16 Monday

17 Tuesday

Patrick, Bishop, Missionary, Patron of Ireland

Bank Holiday

(N. Ireland and Rep. of Ireland)

Wednesday **18**

Thursday **19**

Joseph of Nazareth (*CW*)

Friday **20**

Saturday **21**

March 2026

22 Sunday

The Fifth Sunday of Lent
5 in Lent

23 Monday

24 Tuesday

Wednesday **25**

THE ANNUNCIATION OF OUR LORD TO THE BLESSED VIRGIN MARY

Thursday **26**

Friday **27**

Saturday **28**

Summer Time
begins tomorrow

March 2026

29 Sunday

Palm Sunday
Summer Time begins

30 Monday

31 Tuesday

Wednesday **1**

MAUNDY THURSDAY Thursday **2**

GOOD FRIDAY Friday **3**
Bank Holiday (England,
N. Ireland, Scotland and Wales)

Easter Eve Saturday **4**

5 Sunday **EASTER DAY**

6 Monday Bank Holiday (England, N. Ireland, Wales and Rep. of Ireland)

7 Tuesday

Wednesday **8**

Thursday **9**

Friday **10**

Saturday **11**

April 2026

12 Sunday **The Second Sunday of Easter**
1 after Easter

13 Monday

14 Tuesday

Wednesday **15**

Thursday **16**

Friday **17**

Saturday **18**

19 Sunday **The Third Sunday of Easter**
2 after Easter

20 Monday

21 Tuesday

Wednesday **22**

George, Martyr, Patron of England

Thursday **23**

Friday **24**

Mark the Evangelist

Saturday **25**

April 2026

26 Sunday

The Fourth Sunday of Easter
3 after Easter

27 Monday

28 Tuesday

Wednesday **29**

Thursday **30**

Philip and James, Apostles Friday **1**

Saturday **2**

May 2026

3 Sunday

The Fifth Sunday of Easter
4 after Easter

4 Monday

Bank Holiday (England, N. Ireland, Scotland, Wales and Rep. of Ireland)

5 Tuesday

Wednesday **6**

Thursday **7**

Friday **8**

Saturday **9**

10 Sunday **The Sixth Sunday of Easter**
5 after Easter

11 Monday Rogation Day

12 Tuesday Rogation Day

Rogation Day — Wednesday **13**

ASCENSION DAY — Thursday **14**

Matthias the Apostle (*CW*)
(BCP 24 February) — Friday **15**

Saturday **16**

17 Sunday **The Seventh Sunday of Easter**
Sunday after Ascension Day

18 Monday

19 Tuesday

Wednesday **20**

Thursday **21**

Friday **22**

Saturday **23**

May 2026

24 Sunday

DAY OF PENTECOST
WHIT SUNDAY

25 Monday

Bank Holiday (England, N. Ireland, Scotland and Wales)

26 Tuesday

Ember Day (BCP) Wednesday **27**

Thursday **28**

Ember Day (BCP) Friday **29**

Ember Day (BCP) Saturday **30**

31 Sunday **TRINITY SUNDAY**

1 Monday Bank Holiday (Rep. of Ireland)
The Visit of the Blessed Virgin Mary to Elizabeth (*CW*)

2 Tuesday

Wednesday **3**

Thursday **4**

Day of Thanksgiving for Holy Communion (Corpus Christi) (*CW*)

Friday **5**

Saturday **6**

7 Sunday

The First Sunday after Trinity
1 after Trinity

8 Monday

9 Tuesday

Wednesday **10**

Barnabas the Apostle Thursday **11**

Friday **12**

Saturday **13**

June 2026

14 Sunday **The Second Sunday after Trinity**

2 after Trinity

15 Monday

16 Tuesday

Wednesday **17**

Thursday **18**

Friday **19**

Saturday **20**

June 2026

21 Sunday **The Third Sunday after Trinity**

3 after Trinity

22 Monday

23 Tuesday

The Birth of John the Baptist Wednesday **24**
Ember Day (*CW*)

Thursday **25**

Ember Day (*CW*) Friday **26**

Ember Day (*CW*) Saturday **27**

June 2026

28 Sunday **The Fourth Sunday after Trinity**
4 after Trinity

29 Monday **Peter and Paul, Apostles** (CW)
Peter the Apostle (BCP)

30 Tuesday

Wednesday **1**

Thursday **2**

Thomas the Apostle (*CW*)
(BCP 22 December)

Friday **3**

Saturday **4**

July 2026

5 Sunday

The Fifth Sunday after Trinity
5 after Trinity

6 Monday

7 Tuesday

Wednesday **8**

Thursday **9**

Friday **10**

Saturday **11**

12 Sunday

The Sixth Sunday after Trinity
6 after Trinity

13 Monday

Bank Holiday
(N. Ireland)

14 Tuesday

Wednesday **15**

Thursday **16**

Friday **17**

Saturday **18**

July 2026

19 Sunday **The Seventh Sunday after Trinity**
7 after Trinity

20 Monday

21 Tuesday

Mary Magdalene Wednesday **22**

Thursday **23**

Friday **24**

James the Apostle Saturday **25**

July 2026

26 Sunday **The Eighth Sunday after Trinity**

8 after Trinity

27 Monday

28 Tuesday

Wednesday **29**

Thursday **30**

Friday **31**

Saturday **1**

August 2026

2 Sunday

The Ninth Sunday after Trinity
9 after Trinity

3 Monday

Bank Holiday
(Scotland and Rep. of Ireland)

4 Tuesday

Wednesday **5**

The Transfiguration of Our Lord Thursday **6**

Friday **7**

Saturday **8**

August 2026

9 Sunday **The Tenth Sunday after Trinity**

10 after Trinity

10 Monday

11 Tuesday

Wednesday **12**

Thursday **13**

Friday **14**

The Blessed Virgin Mary (*CW*) Saturday **15**

August 2026

16 Sunday **The Eleventh Sunday after Trinity**

11 after Trinity

17 Monday

18 Tuesday

Wednesday **19**

Thursday **20**

Friday **21**

Saturday **22**

August 2026

23 Sunday **The Twelfth Sunday after Trinity**
12 after Trinity

24 Monday **Bartholomew the Apostle**

25 Tuesday

Wednesday **26**

Thursday **27**

Friday **28**

Saturday **29**

30 Sunday **The Thirteenth Sunday after Trinity**
13 after Trinity

31 Monday Bank Holiday (England, N. Ireland and Wales)

1 Tuesday

September 2026

Wednesday **2**

Thursday **3**

Friday **4**

Saturday **5**

September 2026

6 Sunday **The Fourteenth Sunday after Trinity**
14 after Trinity

7 Monday

8 Tuesday The King's Accession (in 2022)

Wednesday **9**

Thursday **10**

Friday **11**

Saturday **12**

September 2026

13 Sunday **The Fifteenth Sunday after Trinity**
15 after Trinity
Education Sunday

14 Monday **Holy Cross Day**

15 Tuesday

Ember Day (BCP) Wednesday **16**

Thursday **17**

Ember Day (BCP) Friday **18**

Ember Day (BCP) Saturday **19**

September 2026

20 Sunday **The Sixteenth Sunday after Trinity**
16 after Trinity

21 Monday **Matthew, Apostle and Evangelist**

22 Tuesday

Ember Day (CW) Wednesday **23**

Thursday **24**

Ember Day (CW) Friday **25**

Ember Day (CW) Saturday **26**

September 2026

27 Sunday **The Seventeenth Sunday after Trinity**

17 after Trinity

28 Monday

29 Tuesday **Michael and All Angels**

Wednesday **30**

Thursday **1**

Friday **2**

Saturday **3**

October 2026

4 Sunday **The Eighteenth Sunday after Trinity**
18 after Trinity

5 Monday

6 Tuesday

Wednesday **7**

Thursday **8**

Friday **9**

Saturday **10**

11 Sunday **The Nineteenth Sunday after Trinity**

19 after Trinity

12 Monday

13 Tuesday

Wednesday **14**

Thursday **15**

Friday **16**

Saturday **17**

October 2026

18 Sunday

The Twentieth Sunday after Trinity
20 after Trinity
Luke the Evangelist

19 Monday

20 Tuesday

Wednesday **21**

Thursday **22**

Friday **23**

Summer Time
ends tomorrow

Saturday **24**

October 2026

25 Sunday

The Last Sunday after Trinity
21 after Trinity
Bible Sunday
Summer Time ends

26 Monday

Bank Holiday (Rep. of Ireland)

27 Tuesday

Simon and Jude, Apostles Wednesday **28**

Thursday **29**

Friday **30**

Saturday **31**

November 2026

1 Sunday **ALL SAINTS' DAY**

2 Monday

3 Tuesday

Wednesday **4**

Thursday **5**

Friday **6**

Saturday **7**

November 2026

8 Sunday

The Third Sunday before Advent
23 after Trinity
Remembrance Sunday

9 Monday

10 Tuesday

Wednesday **11**

Thursday **12**

Friday **13**

Saturday **14**

November 2026

15 Sunday **The Second Sunday before Advent**
24 after Trinity

16 Monday

17 Tuesday

Wednesday **18**

Thursday **19**

Friday **20**

Saturday **21**

November 2026

22 Sunday

Christ the King

Sunday next before Advent

23 Monday

24 Tuesday

Wednesday **25**

Thursday **26**

Friday **27**

Saturday **28**

Nov/Dec 2026

29 Sunday — **The First Sunday of Advent**
1 in Advent

30 Monday — **Andrew the Apostle**
Bank Holiday (Scotland)

1 Tuesday

Wednesday **2**

Thursday **3**

Friday **4**

Saturday **5**

December 2026

6 Sunday **The Second Sunday of Advent**
2 in Advent

7 Monday

8 Tuesday

Ember Day (CW) Wednesday **9**

Thursday **10**

Ember Day (CW) Friday **11**

Ember Day (CW) Saturday **12**

December 2026

13 Sunday **The Third Sunday of Advent**
3 in Advent

14 Monday

15 Tuesday

Ember Day (BCP) Wednesday **16**

Thursday **17**

Ember Day (BCP) Friday **18**

Ember Day (BCP) Saturday **19**

December 2026

20 Sunday **The Fourth Sunday of Advent**
4 in Advent

21 Monday **Thomas the Apostle** (BCP)
(*CW* 3 July)

22 Tuesday

Wednesday **23**

Christmas Eve

Thursday **24**

CHRISTMAS DAY
Bank Holiday (England, N. Ireland, Scotland, Wales and Rep. of Ireland)

Friday **25**

Stephen, Deacon, First Martyr

Saturday **26**

December 2026

27 Sunday

The First Sunday of Christmas
Sunday after Christmas Day
John, Apostle and Evangelist

28 Monday

The Holy Innocents
Bank Holiday (England, N. Ireland, Scotland, Wales and Rep. of Ireland)

29 Tuesday

Wednesday **30**

Thursday **31**

Friday **1**

The Naming and Circumcision of Jesus (*CW*)
The Circumcision of Christ (BCP)
Bank Holiday (England, N. Ireland, Scotland, Wales and Rep. of Ireland)

Saturday **2**

January 2027

3 Sunday **The Second Sunday of Christmas**
2 after Christmas

4 Monday Bank Holiday (Scotland)

5 Tuesday

Reminders for 2027

January

February

Reminders for 2027

March

April

Reminders for 2027

May

June

Reminders for 2027

July

August

September

October

Reminders for 2027

November

December

Memoranda

Notes on the Lectionary

Making choices in *Common Worship*

Common Worship makes provision for a variety of pastoral and liturgical circumstances. It needs to, for it has to serve some church communities where Morning Prayer, Holy Communion and Evening Prayer are all celebrated every day, and yet be useful also in a church with only one service a week, and that service varying in form and time from week to week.

At the beginning of the year, some decisions in principle need to be taken.

In relation to the Calendar, whether to keep The Epiphany on Tuesday 6 January or on Sunday 4 January, and whether to keep The Presentation of Christ (Candlemas) on Monday 2 February or on Sunday 1 February.

In relation to the Lectionary

The initial choices every year to decide in relation to Sundays are:

- which of the services on a Principal Feast, Principal Holy Day, Sunday or Festival constitutes the 'Principal Service'; then use the Principal Service Lectionary (column 3) consistently for that service through the year;
- during the Sundays after Trinity, whether to use Track I of the Principal Service Lectionary (column 2), where the first reading stays over several weeks with one Old Testament book read semi-continuously, or Track 2 (column 3), where the first reading is chosen for its relationship to the Gospel reading of the day;
- which, if any, service on a Principal Feast, Principal Holy Day, Sunday or Festival constitutes the 'Second Service'; then use the Second Service Lectionary (column 5) consistently for that service through the year;
- which, if any, service on a Principal Feast, Principal Holy Day, Sunday or Festival constitutes the 'Third Service'; then use the Third Service Lectionary (column 4) consistently for that service through the year.

In relation to weekdays

- whether to use the Daily Eucharistic Lectionary (column 3) consistently for weekday celebrations of Holy Communion (with the exception of Principal Feasts, Principal Holy Days and Festivals) or to make some use of the Lesser Festival provision;
- whether to follow the first psalm provision in column 4 (morning) and column 5 (evening), where psalms during the seasons have a seasonal flavour but in ordinary time follow a sequential pattern; or to follow the alternative provision in the same columns, where psalms follow the sequential pattern throughout the year, except for the period between 19 December and The Epiphany and from the Monday of Holy Week to the Saturday of Easter Week; or to follow the psalm cycle in the Book of Common Prayer, where they are nearly always used 'in course'.

The flexibility of *Common Worship* is intended to enable the church and the minister to find the most helpful provision for them. But once a decision is made, it is advisable to stay with that decision through the year or at the very least through a complete season.

November/ December 2025		Sunday Principal Service Weekday Eucharist	Third Service Morning Prayer	Second Service Evening Prayer
30 Sunday	**THE FIRST SUNDAY OF ADVENT** (Andrew transferred to 1 December) *Common Worship* Year A begins			
P		Isa. 2. 1–5 Ps. 122 Rom. 13. 11–end Matt. 24. 36–44	Ps. 44 Mic. 4. 1–7 1 Thess. 5. 1–11	Ps. 9 (*or* 9. 1–8) Isa. 52. 1–12 Matt. 24. 15–28 *or First EP of Andrew the Apostle* Ps. 48 Isa. 49. 1–9a 1 Cor. 4. 9–16 **R ct**

December 2025

1 Monday	**ANDREW THE APOSTLE**			
R		Isa. 52. 7–10 Ps. 19. 1–6 Rom. 10. 12–18 Matt. 4. 18–22	*MP*: Ps. 47; 147. 1–12 Ezek. 47. 1–12 *or* Ecclus. 14. 20–end John 12. 20–32	*EP*: Ps. 87; 96 Zech. 8. 20–end John 1. 35–42

2 Tuesday	Daily Eucharistic Lectionary Year 2 begins		
P	Isa. 11. 1–10 Ps. 72. 1–4, 18–19 Luke 10. 21–24	Ps. ***80***; 82 *alt.* Ps. ***5***; 6; (8) Isa. 26. 1–13 Matt. 12. 22–37	Ps. ***74***; 75 *alt.* Ps. ***9***; 10† Isa. 43. 1–13 Rev. ch. 20
3 Wednesday	*Francis Xavier, Missionary, Apostle of the Indies, 1552*		
P	Isa. 25. 6–10a Ps. 23 Matt. 15. 29–37	Ps. 5; ***7*** *alt.* Ps. 119. 1–32 Isa. 28. 1–13 Matt. 12. 38–end	Ps. 76; ***77*** *alt.* Ps. ***11***; 12; 13 Isa. 43. 14–end Rev. 21. 1–8
4 Thursday	*John of Damascus, Monk, Teacher, c. 749; Nicholas Ferrar, Deacon, Founder of the Little Gidding Community, 1637*		
P	Isa. 26. 1–6 Ps. 118. 18–27a Matt. 7. 21, 24–27	Ps. ***42***; 43 *alt.* Ps. 14; ***15***; 16 Isa. 28. 14–end Matt. 13. 1–23	Ps. ***40***; 46 *alt.* Ps. 18† Isa. 44. 1–8 Rev. 21. 9–21
5 Friday			
P	Isa. 29. 17–end Ps. 27. 1–4, 16–17 Matt. 9. 27–31	Ps. ***25***; 26 *alt.* Ps. 17; ***19*** Isa. 29. 1–14 Matt. 13. 24–43	Ps. 16; ***17*** *alt.* Ps. 22 Isa. 44. 9–23 Rev. 21.22 – 22.5

December 2025			Sunday Principal Service Weekday Eucharist	Third Service Morning Prayer	Second Service Evening Prayer
6 Saturday	**Nicholas, Bishop of Myra, c. 326**				
Pw	Com. Bishop *also* Isa. 61. 1–3 1 Tim. 6. 6–11 Mark 10. 13–16	*or*	Isa. 30. 19–21, 23–26 Ps. 146. 4–9 Matt. 9.35 – 10.1, 6–8	Ps. ***9***; 10 *alt.* Ps. 20; 21; ***23*** Isa. 29. 15–end Matt. 13. 44–end	Ps. ***27***; 28 *alt.* Ps. ***24***; 25 Isa. 44.24 – 45.13 Rev. 22. 6–end **ct**
7 Sunday	**THE SECOND SUNDAY OF ADVENT**				
P			Isa. 11. 1–10 Ps. 72. 1–7, 18–19 (*or* 72. 1–7) Rom. 15. 4–13 Matt. 3. 1–12	Ps. 80 Amos ch. 7 Luke 1. 5–20	Ps. 11; [28] 1 Kings 18. 17–39 John 1. 19–28
8 Monday	**The Conception of the Blessed Virgin Mary**				
Pw	Com. BVM	*or*	Isa. ch. 35 Ps. 85. 7–end Luke 5. 17–26	Ps. 44 *alt.* Ps. 27; ***30*** Isa. 30. 1–18 Matt. 14. 1–12	Ps. ***144***; 146 *alt.* Ps. 26; ***28***; 29 Isa. 45. 14–end 1 Thess. ch. 1

9 Tuesday				
	P	Isa. 40. 1–11 Ps. 96. 1, 10–end Matt. 18. 12–14	Ps. ***56***; 57 *alt.* Ps. 32; ***36*** Isa. 30. 19–end Matt. 14. 13–end	Ps. ***11***; 12; 13 *alt.* Ps. 33 Isa. ch. 46 1 Thess. 2. 1–12
10 Wednesday Ember Day				
	P	Isa. 40. 25–end Ps. 103. 8–13 Matt. 11. 28–end	Ps. ***62***; 63 *alt.* Ps. 34 Isa. ch. 31 Matt. 15. 1–20	Ps. ***10***; 14 *alt.* Ps. 119. 33–56 Isa. ch. 47 1 Thess. 2. 13–end
11 Thursday				
	P	Isa. 41. 13–20 Ps. 145. 1, 8–13 Matt. 11. 11–15	Ps. 53; ***54***; 60 *alt.* Ps. 37† Isa. ch. 32 Matt. 15. 21–28	Ps. 73 *alt.* Ps. 39; ***40*** Isa. 48. 1–11 1 Thess. ch. 3
12 Friday Ember Day				
	P	Isa. 48. 17–19 Ps. 1 Matt. 11. 16–19	Ps. 85; ***86*** *alt.* Ps. 31 Isa. 33. 1–22 Matt. 15. 29–end	Ps. 82; ***90*** *alt.* Ps. 35 Isa. 48. 12–end 1 Thess. 4. 1–12

December 2025		Sunday Principal Service Weekday Eucharist	Third Service Morning Prayer	Second Service Evening Prayer
13 Saturday	**Lucy, Martyr at Syracuse, 304** Ember Day* *Samuel Johnson, Moralist, 1784*			
Pr	Com. Martyr *also* Wisd. 3. 1–7 2 Cor. 4. 6–15 *or*	Ecclus. 48. 1–4, 9–11 *or* 2 Kings 2. 9–12 Ps. 80. 1–4, 18–19 Matt. 17. 10–13	Ps. 145 *alt.* Ps. 41; **42**; 43 Isa. ch. 35 Matt. 16. 1–12	Ps. 93; ***94*** *alt.* Ps. 45; ***46*** Isa. 49. 1–13 1 Thess. 4. 13–end **ct**
14 Sunday	**THE THIRD SUNDAY OF ADVENT**			
P		Isa. 35. 1–10 Ps. 146. 4–10 *or Canticle*: Magnificat James 5. 7–10 Matt. 11. 2–11	Ps. 68. 1–19 Zeph. 3. 14–end Phil. 4. 4–7	Ps. 12; [14] Isa. 5. 8–end Acts 13. 13–41 *Gospel*: John 5. 31–40
15 Monday				
P		Num. 24. 2–7, 15–17 Ps. 25. 3–8 Matt. 21. 23–27	Ps. 40 *alt.* Ps. 44 Isa. 38. 1–8, 21–22 Matt. 16. 13–end	Ps. 25; ***26*** *alt.* Ps. ***47***; 49 Isa. 49. 14–25 1 Thess. 5. 1–11

16 Tuesday			
P	Zeph. 3. 1–2, 9–13 Ps. 34. 1–6, 21–22 Matt. 21. 28–32	Ps. ***70***; 74 *alt*. Ps. ***48***; 52 Isa. 38. 9–20 Matt. 17. 1–13	Ps. ***50***; 54 *alt*. Ps. 50 Isa. ch. 50 1 Thess. 5. 12–end
17 Wednesday	O Sapientia *Eglantyne Jebb, Social Reformer, Founder of 'Save the Children', 1928*		
P	Gen. 49. 2, 8–10 Ps. 72. 1–5, 18–19 Matt. 1. 1–17	Ps. ***75***; 96 *alt*. Ps. 119. 57–80 Isa. ch. 39 Matt. 17. 14–21	Ps. 25; ***82*** *alt*. Ps. ***59***; 60; (67) Isa. 51. 1–8 2 Thess. ch. 1
18 Thursday			
P	Jer. 23. 5–8 Ps. 72. 1–2, 12–13, 18–end Matt. 1. 18–24	Ps. ***76***; 97 *alt*. Ps. 56; ***57***; (63†) Zeph. 1.1 – 2.3 Matt. 17. 22–end	Ps. 44 *alt*. Ps. 61; ***62***; 64 Isa. 51. 9–16 2 Thess. ch. 2
19 Friday			
P	Judg. 13. 2–7, 24–end Ps. 71. 3–8 Luke 1. 5–25	Ps. 144; ***146*** Zeph. 3. 1–13 Matt. 18. 1–20	Ps. 10; ***57*** Isa. 51. 17–end 2 Thess. ch. 3

December 2025		Sunday Principal Service Weekday Eucharist	Third Service Morning Prayer	Second Service Evening Prayer
20 Saturday				
P		Isa. 7. 10–14 Ps. 24. 1–6 Luke 1. 26–38	Ps. ***46***; 95 Zeph. 3. 14–end Matt. 18. 21–end	Ps. ***4***; 9 Isa. 52. 1–12 Jude **ct**
21 Sunday	**THE FOURTH SUNDAY OF ADVENT**			
P		Isa. 7. 10–16 Ps. 80. 1–8, 18–20 (*or* 80. 1–8) Rom. 1. 1–7 Matt. 1. 18–end	Ps. 144 Mic. 5. 2–5a Luke 1. 26–38	Ps. 113; [126] 1 Sam. 1. 1–20 Rev. 22. 6–end *Gospel*: Luke 1. 39–45
22 Monday*				
P		1 Sam. 1. 24–end Ps. 113 Luke 1. 46–56	Ps. ***124***; 125; 126; 127 Mal. 1. 1, 6–end Matt. 19. 1–12	Ps. 24; ***48*** Isa. 52.13 – 53.end 1 Pet. 1. 1–15

23 Tuesday

P	Mal. 3. 1–4; 4. 5–end Ps. 25. 3–9 Luke 1. 57–66	Ps. 128; 129; ***130***; 131 Mal. 2. 1–16 Matt. 19. 13–15	Ps. 89. 1–37 Isa. ch. 54 2 Pet. 1.16 – 2.3

24 Wednesday **CHRISTMAS EVE**

P	*Morning Eucharist* 2 Sam. 7. 1–5, 8–11, 16 Ps. 89. 2, 19–27 Acts 13. 16–26 Luke 1. 67–79	Ps. ***45***; 113 Mal. 2.17 – 3.12 Matt. 19. 16–end	Ps. 85 Zech. ch. 2 Rev. 1. 1–8

*Thomas the Apostle may be celebrated on 22 December instead of 3 July in 2025.

December 2025		Sunday Principal Service Weekday Eucharist	Third Service Morning Prayer	Second Service Evening Prayer
25 Thursday	**CHRISTMAS DAY**			
𝔚	*Any of the following sets of readings may be used on the evening of Christmas Eve and on Christmas Day. Set III should be used at some service during the celebration.*	*I* Isa. 9. 2–7 Ps. 96 Titus 2. 11–14 Luke 2. 1–14 [15–20] *II* Isa. 62. 6–end Ps. 97 Titus 3. 4–7 Luke 2. [1–7] 8–20 *III* Isa. 52. 7–10 Ps. 98 Heb. 1. 1–4 [5–12] John 1. 1–14	*MP*: Ps. ***110***; 117 Isa. 62. 1–5 Matt. 1. 18–end	*EP*: Ps. 8 Isa. 65. 17–25 Phil. 2. 5–11 *or* Luke 2. 1–20 *if it has not been used at the principal service of the day*

26 Friday	**STEPHEN, DEACON, FIRST MARTYR**			
R		2 Chron. 24. 20–22 *or* Acts 7. 51–end Ps. 119. 161–168 Acts 7. 51–end *or* Gal. 2. 16b–20 Matt. 10. 17–22	*MP*: Ps. ***13***; 31. 1–8; 150 Jer. 26. 12–15 Acts ch. 6	*EP*: Ps. 57; **86** Gen. 4. 1–10 Matt. 23. 34–end
27 Saturday	**JOHN, APOSTLE AND EVANGELIST**			
W		Exod. 33. 7–11a Ps. 117 1 John ch. 1 John 21. 19b–end	*MP*: Ps. ***21***; 147. 13–end Exod. 33. 12–end 1 John 2. 1–11	*EP*: Ps. 97 Isa. 6. 1–8 1 John 5. 1–12
28 Sunday	**THE HOLY INNOCENTS** (or transferred to 29 December)			
R		Jer. 31. 15–17 Ps. 124 1 Cor. 1. 26–29 Matt. 2. 13–18	*MP*: Ps. **36**; 146 Baruch 4. 21–27 *or* Gen. 37. 13–20 Matt. 18. 1–10	*EP*: Ps. 123; ***128*** Isa. 49. 14–25 Mark 10. 13–16
	or, for The First Sunday of Christmas:			
W		Isa. 63. 7–9 Ps. 148 (*or* 148. 7–end) Heb. 2. 10–end Matt. 2. 13–end	Ps. 105. 1–11 Isa. 35. 1–6 Gal. 3. 23–end	Ps. 132 Isa. 49. 7–13 Phil. 2. 1–11 *Gospel*: Luke 2. 41–52

December 2025/ January 2026		Sunday Principal Service Weekday Eucharist	Third Service Morning Prayer	Second Service Evening Prayer
29 Monday	**Thomas Becket, Archbishop of Canterbury, Martyr, 1170***			
Wr	Com. Martyr *esp.* Matt. 10. 28–33 *also* Ecclus. 51. 1–8	*or* 1 John 2. 3–11 Ps. 96. 1–4 Luke 2. 22–35	Ps. ***19***; 20 Jonah ch. 1 Col. 1. 1–14	Ps. 131; ***132*** Isa. 57. 15–end John 1. 1–18
30 Tuesday				
W		1 John 2. 12–17 Ps. 96. 7–10 Luke 2. 36–40	Ps. 111; 112; ***113*** Jonah ch. 2 Col. 1. 15–23	Ps. ***65***; 84 Isa. 59. 1–15a John 1. 19–28
31 Wednesday	*John Wyclif, Reformer, 1384*			
W		1 John 2. 18–21 Ps. 96. 1, 11–end John 1. 1–18	Ps. 102 Jonah chs 3 & 4 Col. 1.24 – 2.7	Ps. ***90***; 148 Isa. 59. 15b–end John 1. 29–34 *or First EP of The Naming of Jesus* Ps. 148 Jer. 23. 1–6 Col. 2. 8–15 **ct**

January 2026

1 Thursday	**THE NAMING AND CIRCUMCISION OF JESUS**				
W			Num. 6. 22–end Ps. 8 Gal. 4. 4–7 Luke 2. 15–21	*MP*: Ps. ***103***; 150 Gen. 17. 1–13 Rom. 2. 17–end	*EP*: Ps. 115 Deut. 30. [1–10] 11–end Acts 3. 1–16
2 Friday	**Basil the Great and Gregory of Nazianzus, Bishops, Teachers, 379 and 389** *Seraphim, Monk of Sarov, Spiritual Guide, 1833; Vedanayagam Samuel Azariah, Bishop in South India, Evangelist, 1945*				
W	Com. Teacher *esp.* 2 Tim. 4. 1–8 Matt. 5. 13–19	*or*	1 John 2. 22–28 Ps. 98. 1–4 John 1. 19–28	Ps. 18. 1–30 Ruth ch. 1 Col. 2. 8–end	Ps. 45; ***46*** Isa. 60. 1–12 John 1. 35–42
3 Saturday					
W			1 John 2.29 – 3.6 Ps. 98. 2–7 John 1. 29–34	Ps. ***127***; 128; 131 Ruth ch. 2 Col. 3. 1–11	Ps. **2**; 110 Isa. 60. 13–end John 1. 43–end

*Thomas Becket may be celebrated on 7 July instead of 29 December in 2025.

January 2026		Sunday Principal Service Weekday Eucharist	Third Service Morning Prayer	Second Service Evening Prayer
4 Sunday	**THE SECOND SUNDAY OF CHRISTMAS** *or* The Epiphany (*see provision on 5 and 6 January*)			
W		Jer. 31. 7–14 *or* Ecclus. 24. 1–12 Ps. 147. 13–end *or Canticle*: Wisd. 10. 15–end Eph. 1. 3–14 John 1. [1–9] 10–18	Ps. 87 Jer. 31. 15–17 2 Cor. 1. 3–12	Ps. 135 (*or* 135. 1–14) Isa. 41.21 – 42.4 Col. 1. 1–14 *Gospel*: Matt. 2. 13–end
5 Monday				
W		1 John 3. 11–21 Ps. 100 John 1. 43–end	Ps. 8; ***48*** Ruth 4. 1–17 Col. 4. 2–end	*First EP of The Epiphany* Ps. 96; ***97*** Isa. 49. 1–13 John 4. 7–26 **𝔚 ct**
	or, if The Epiphany is celebrated on 4 January:	1 John 3.22 – 4.6 Ps. 2. 7–end Matt. 4. 12–17, 23–end	Ps. 8; ***48*** *alt*. Ps. 71 Ruth ch. 3 Col. 3.12 – 4.1	Ps. 96; ***97*** *alt*. Ps. ***72***; 75 Isa. ch. 61 John 2. 1–12

6 Tuesday	**THE EPIPHANY**		
𝔚	Isa. 60. 1–6 Ps. 72 (*or* 72. 10–15) Eph. 3. 1–12 Matt. 2. 1–12	*MP*: Ps. ***132***; 113 Jer. 31. 7–14 John 1. 29–34	*EP*: Ps. **98**; 100 Baruch 4.36 – 5.end *or* Isa. 60. 1–9 John 2. 1–11
	or, if The Epiphany is celebrated on 4 January: 1 John 4. 7–10 Ps. 72. 1–8 Mark 6. 34–44	Ps. 89. 1–37 *alt*. Ps. 73 Ruth 4. 1–17 Col. 4. 2–end	Ps. 85; ***87*** *alt*. Ps. 74 Isa. ch. 62 John 2. 13–end
7 Wednesday			
W	1 John 3.22 – 4.6 Ps. 2. 7–end Matt. 4. 12–17, 23–end	***99***; 147. 1–12 *alt*. Ps. 77 Baruch 1.15 – 2.10 *or* Jer. 23. 1–8 Matt. 20. 1–16	Ps. 118 *alt*. Ps. 119. 81–104 Isa. 63. 7–end 1 John ch. 3
	or, if The Epiphany is celebrated on 4 January: 1 John 4. 11–18 Ps. 72. 1, 10–13 Mark 6. 45–52	Ps. ***99***; 147. 1–12 *alt*. Ps. 77 Baruch 1.15 – 2.10 *or* Jer. 23. 1–8 Matt. 20. 1–16	Ps. 118 *alt*. Ps. 119. 81–104 Isa. 63. 7–end 1 John ch. 3

		Sunday Principal Service Weekday Eucharist	Third Service Morning Prayer	Second Service Evening Prayer
8 Thursday				
W		1 John 4. 7–10 Ps. 72. 1–8 Mark 6. 34–44	Ps. ***46***; 147. 13–end *alt*. Ps. 78. 1–39† Baruch 2. 11–end *or* Jer. 30. 1–17 Matt. 20. 17–28	Ps. 145 *alt*. Ps. 78. 40–end† Isa. ch. 64 1 John 4. 7–end
	or, if The Epiphany is celebrated on 4 January:			
		1 John 4.19 – 5.4 Ps. 72. 1, 17–end Luke 4. 14–22	Ps. ***46***; 147. 13–end *alt*. Ps. 78. 1–39† Baruch 2. 11–end *or* Jer. 30. 1–17 Matt. 20. 17–28	Ps. 145 *alt*. Ps. 78. 40–end† Isa. ch. 64 1 John 4. 7–end

9 Friday

W	1 John 4. 11–18 Ps. 72. 1, 10–13 Mark 6. 45–52	Ps. 2; ***148*** *alt.* Ps. 55 Baruch 3. 1–8 *or* Jer. 30.18 – 31.9 Matt. 20. 29–end	Ps. ***67***; 72 *alt.* Ps. 69 Isa. 65. 1–16 1 John 5. 1–12

or, if The Epiphany is celebrated on 4 January:

	1 John 5. 5–13 Ps. 147. 13–end Luke 5. 12–16	Ps. 2; ***148*** *alt.* Ps. 55 Baruch 3. 1–8 *or* Jer. 30.18 – 31.9 Matt. 20. 29–end	Ps. ***67***; 72 *alt.* Ps. 69 Isa. 65. 1–16 1 John 5. 1–12

January 2026		Sunday Principal Service Weekday Eucharist	Third Service Morning Prayer	Second Service Evening Prayer
10 Saturday	*William Laud, Archbishop of Canterbury, 1645*			
W		1 John 4.19 - 5.4 Ps. 72. 1, 17–end Luke 4. 14–22	Ps. 97; ***149*** *alt.* Ps. ***76***; 79 Baruch 3.9 - 4.4 *or* Jer. 31. 10–17 Matt. 23. 1–12	Ps. 27; ***29*** *alt.* Ps. 81; ***84*** Isa. 65. 17–end 1 John 5. 13–end *or First EP of The Baptism* Ps. 36 Isa. ch. 61 Titus 2. 11–14; 3. 4–7 **𝔚 ct**
	or, if The Epiphany is celebrated on 4 January:			
		1 John 5. 14–end Ps. 149. 1–5 John 3. 22–30	Ps. 97; ***149*** *alt.* Ps. ***76***; 79 Isa. 65. 1–16 1 John 5. 1–12	Ps. 27; ***29*** *alt.* Ps. 81; ***84*** Isa. 65. 17–end 1 John 5. 13–end *or First EP of The Baptism* Ps. 36 Isa. ch. 61 Titus 2. 11–14; 3. 4–7 **𝔚 ct**

11 Sunday	**THE BAPTISM OF CHRIST (THE FIRST SUNDAY OF EPIPHANY)**				
𝖂			Isa. 42. 1–9 Ps. 29 Acts 10. 34–43 Matt. 3. 13–end	Ps. 89. 19–29 Exod. 14. 15–22 1 John 5. 6–9	Ps. 46; 47 Josh. 3. 1–8, 14–end Heb. 1. 1–12 *Gospel*: Luke 3. 15–22
12 Monday	**Aelred of Hexham, Abbot of Rievaulx, 1167** *Benedict Biscop, Abbot of Wearmouth, Scholar, 689*				
W **DEL 1**	Com. Religious *also* Ecclus. 15. 1–6	*or*	1 Sam. 1. 1–8 Ps. 116. 10–15 Mark 1. 14–20	Ps. **2**; 110 *alt.* Ps. ***80***; 82 Gen. 1. 1–19 Matt. 21. 1–17	Ps. **34**; 36 *alt.* Ps. ***85***; 86 Amos ch. 1 1 Cor. 1. 1–17
13 Tuesday	**Hilary, Bishop of Poitiers, Teacher, 367** *Kentigern (Mungo), Missionary Bishop in Strathclyde and Cumbria, 603; George Fox, Founder of the Society of Friends (the Quakers), 1691*				
W	Com. Teacher *also* 1 John 2. 18–25 John 8. 25–32	*or*	1 Sam. 1. 9–20 *Canticle*: 1 Sam. 2. 1, 4–8 *or* Magnificat Mark 1. 21–28	Ps. 8; ***9*** *alt.* Ps. 87; ***89. 1–18*** Gen. 1.20 – 2.3 Matt. 21. 18–32	Ps. ***45***; 46 *alt.* Ps. 89. 19–end Amos ch. 2 1 Cor. 1. 18–end

January 2026		Sunday Principal Service Weekday Eucharist	Third Service Morning Prayer	Second Service Evening Prayer
14 Wednesday				
W		1 Sam. 3. 1–10, 19–20 Ps. 40. 1–4, 7–10 Mark 1. 29–39	Ps. 19; ***20*** *alt*. Ps. 119. 105–128 Gen. 2. 4–end Matt. 21. 33–end	Ps. ***47***; 48 *alt*. Ps. ***91***; 93 Amos ch. 3 1 Cor. ch. 2
15 Thursday				
W		1 Sam. 4. 1–11 Ps. 44. 10–15, 24–25 Mark 1. 40–end	Ps. ***21***; 24 *alt*. Ps. 90; ***92*** Gen. ch. 3 Matt. 22. 1–14	Ps. ***61***; 65 *alt*. Ps. 94 Amos ch. 4 1 Cor. ch. 3
16 Friday				
W		1 Sam. 8. 4–7, 10–end Ps. 89. 15–18 Mark 2. 1–12	Ps. ***67***; 72 *alt*. Ps. ***88***; (95) Gen. 4. 1–16, 25–26 Matt. 22. 15–33	Ps. 68 *alt*. Ps. 102 Amos 5. 1–17 1 Cor. ch. 4

17 Saturday	**Antony of Egypt, Hermit, Abbot, 356** *Charles Gore, Bishop, Founder of the Community of the Resurrection, 1932*				
W	Com. Religious *esp*. Phil. 3. 7–14 *also* Matt. 19. 16–26	*or*	1 Sam. 9. 1–4, 17–19; 10. 1a Ps. 21. 1–6 Mark 2. 13–17	Ps. 29; ***33*** *alt*. Ps. 96; ***97***; 100 Gen. 6. 1–10 Matt. 22. 34–end	Ps. 84; ***85*** *alt*. Ps. 104 Amos 5. 18–end 1 Cor. ch. 5 **ct**
18 Sunday	**THE SECOND SUNDAY OF EPIPHANY** The Week of Prayer for Christian Unity until 25 January				
W			Isa. 49. 1–7 Ps. 40. 1–12 1 Cor. 1. 1–9 John 1. 29–42	Ps. 145. 1–12 Jer. 1. 4–10 Mark 1. 14–20	Ps. 96 Ezek. 2.1 – 3.4 Gal. 1. 11–end *Gospel*: John 1. 43–end
19 Monday	**Wulfstan, Bishop of Worcester, 1095**				
W **DEL 2**	Com. Bishop *esp*. Matt. 24. 42–46	*or*	1 Sam. 15. 16–23 Ps. 50. 8–10, 16–17, 24 Mark 2. 18–22	Ps. 145; ***146*** *alt*. Ps. ***98***; 99; 101 Gen. 6.11 – 7.10 Matt. 24. 1–14	Ps. 71 *alt*. Ps. 105† (*or* Ps. 103) Amos ch. 6 1 Cor. 6. 1–11

January 2026		Sunday Principal Service Weekday Eucharist	Third Service Morning Prayer	Second Service Evening Prayer
20 Tuesday	*Richard Rolle of Hampole, Spiritual Writer, 1349*			
W		1 Sam. 16. 1–13 Ps. 89. 19–27 Mark 2. 23–end	Ps. ***132***; 147. 1–12 *alt.* Ps. 106† (*or* Ps. 103) Gen. 7. 11–end Matt. 24. 15–28	Ps. 89. 1–37 *alt.* Ps. 107† Amos ch. 7 1 Cor. 6. 12–end
21 Wednesday	**Agnes, Child Martyr at Rome, 304**			
Wr	Com. Martyr *also* Rev. 7. 13–end	*or* 1 Sam. 17. 32–33, 37, 40–51 Ps. 144. 1–2, 9–10 Mark 3. 1–6	Ps. ***81***; 147. 13–end *alt.* Ps. 110; ***111***; 112 Gen. 8. 1–14 Matt. 24. 29–end	Ps. ***97***; 98 *alt.* Ps. 119. 129–152 Amos ch. 8 1 Cor. 7. 1–24
22 Thursday	*Vincent of Saragossa, Deacon, first Martyr of Spain, 304*			
W		1 Sam. 18. 6–9; 19. 1–7 Ps. 56. 1–2, 8–end Mark 3. 7–12	Ps. ***76***; 148 *alt.* Ps. 113; ***115*** Gen. 8.15 – 9.7 Matt. 25. 1–13	Ps. 99; 100; ***111*** *alt.* Ps. 114; ***116***; 117 Amos ch. 9 1 Cor. 7. 25–end

23 Friday					
W			1 Sam. 24. 3–22a Ps. 57. 1–2, 8–end Mark 3. 13–19	Ps. ***27***; 149 *alt.* Ps. 139 Gen. 9. 8–19 Matt. 25. 14–30	Ps. 73 *alt.* Ps. ***130***; 131; 137 Hos. 1.1 – 2.1 1 Cor. ch. 8
24 Saturday	**Francis de Sales, Bishop of Geneva, Teacher, 1622**				
W	Com. Teacher *also* Prov. 3. 13–18 John 3. 17–21	*or*	2 Sam. 1. 1–4, 11–12, 17–19, 23–end Ps. 80. 1–6 Mark 3. 20–21	Ps. ***122***; 128; 150 *alt.* Ps. 120; ***121***; 122 Gen. 11. 1–9 Matt. 25. 31–end	Ps. ***61***; 66 *alt.* Ps. 118 Hos. 2. 2–17 1 Cor. 9. 1–14 **ct** *or First EP of The Conversion of Paul* Ps. 149 Isa. 49. 1–13 Acts 22. 3–16 **ct**

January 2026		Sunday Principal Service Weekday Eucharist	Third Service Morning Prayer	Second Service Evening Prayer
25 Sunday	**THE CONVERSION OF PAUL**			
W		Jer. 1. 4–10 *or* Acts 9. 1–22 Ps. 67 Acts 9. 1–22 *or* Gal. 1. 11–16a Matt. 19. 27–end	*MP*: Ps. 66; 147. 13–end Ezek. 3. 22–end Phil. 3. 1–14	*EP*: Ps. 119. 41–56 Ecclus. 39. 1–10 *or* Isa. 56. 1–8 Col. 1.24 – 2.7
	or, for The Third Sunday of Epiphany:			
W		Isa. 9. 1–4 Ps. 27. 1, 4–12 (*or* 27. 1–11) 1 Cor. 1. 10–18 Matt. 4. 12–23	Ps. 113 Amos 3. 1–8 1 John 1. 1–4	Ps. 33 (*or* 33. 1–12) Eccles. 3. 1–11 1 Pet. 1. 3–12 *Gospel*: Luke 4. 14–21
26 Monday	**Timothy and Titus, Companions of Paul** (For Conversion of Paul, see provision on 25 January.)			
W **DEL 3**	Isa. 61. 1–3a Ps. 100 2 Tim. 2. 1–8 *or* Titus 1. 1–5 Luke 10. 1–9	*or* 2 Sam. 5. 1–7, 10 Ps. 89. 19–27 Mark 3. 22–30	Ps. 40; ***108*** *alt.* Ps. 123; 124; 125; ***126*** Gen. 11.27 – 12.9 Matt. 26. 1–16	Ps. ***138***; 144 *alt.* Ps. ***127***; 128; 129 Hos. 2.18 – 3.end 1 Cor. 9. 15–end

27 Tuesday					
W			2 Sam. 6. 12–15, 17–19 Ps. 24. 7–end Mark 3. 31–end	Ps. 34; ***36*** *alt*. Ps. ***132***; 133 Gen. 13. 2–end Matt. 26. 17–35	Ps. 145 *alt*. Ps. (134); ***135*** Hos. 4. 1–16 1 Cor. 10. 1–13
28 Wednesday	**Thomas Aquinas, Priest, Philosopher, Teacher, 1274**				
W	Com. Teacher *esp*. Wisd. 7. 7–10, 15–16 1 Cor. 2. 9–end John 16. 12–15	*or*	2 Sam. 7. 4–17 Ps. 89. 19–27 Mark 4. 1–20	Ps. 45; ***46*** *alt*. Ps. 119. 153–end Gen. ch. 14 Matt. 26. 36–46	Ps. 21; ***29*** *alt*. Ps. 136 Hos. 5. 1–7 1 Cor. 10.14 – 11.1
29 Thursday					
W			2 Sam. 7. 18–19, 24–end Ps. 132. 1–5, 11–15 Mark 4. 21–25	Ps. ***47***; 48 *alt*. Ps. ***143***; 146 Gen. ch. 15 Matt. 26. 47–56	Ps. ***24***; 33 *alt*. Ps. ***138***; 140; 141 Hos. 5.8 – 6.6 1 Cor. 11. 2–16
30 Friday	**Charles, King and Martyr, 1649**				
Wr	Com. Martyr *also* Ecclus. 2. 12–17 1 Tim. 6. 12–16	*or*	2 Sam. 11. 1–10, 13–17 Ps. 51. 1–6, 9 Mark 4. 26–34	Ps. 61; ***65*** *alt*. Ps. 142; ***144*** Gen. ch. 16 Matt. 26. 57–end	Ps. ***67***; 77 *alt*. Ps. 145 Hos. 6.7 – 7.2 1 Cor. 11. 17–end

January/ February 2026		Sunday Principal Service Weekday Eucharist	Third Service Morning Prayer	Second Service Evening Prayer
31 Saturday	*John Bosco, Priest, Founder of the Salesian Teaching Order, 1888*			
W		2 Sam. 12. 1–7, 10–17 Ps. 51. 11–16 Mark 4. 35–end	Ps. 68 *alt.* Ps. 147 Gen. 17. 1–22 Matt. 27. 1–10	Ps. ***72***; 76 *alt.* ***148***; 149; 150 Hos. ch. 8 1 Cor. 12. 1–11 **ct**

February 2026

1 Sunday	**THE FOURTH SUNDAY OF EPIPHANY** *or The Presentation of Christ in the Temple (Candlemas)**			
W		1 Kings 17. 8–16 Ps. 36. 5–10 1 Cor. 1. 18–end John 2. 1–11	Ps. 71. 1–6, 15–17 Hag. 2. 1–9 1 Cor. 3. 10–17	*First EP of The Presentation* Ps. 118 1 Sam. 1. 19b–end Heb. 4. 11–end **𝔚 ct**

2 Monday	**THE PRESENTATION OF CHRIST IN THE TEMPLE (CANDLEMAS)**			
𝔚 **DEL 4**		Mal. 3. 1–5 Ps. 24 (*or* 24. 7–end) Heb. 2. 14–end Luke 2. 22–40	*MP*: Ps. ***48***; 146 Exod. 13. 1–16 Rom. 12. 1–5	*EP*: Ps. 122; ***132*** Hag. 2. 1–9 John 2. 18–22
	or, if The Presentation is observed on 1 February:			
G		2 Sam. 15. 13–14, 30; 16. 5–13 Ps. 3 Mark 5. 1–20	Ps. ***1***; 2; 3 Gen. 18. 1–15 Matt. 27. 11–26	Ps. ***4***; 7 Hos. ch. 9 1 Cor. 12. 12–end

3 Tuesday	**Anskar, Archbishop of Hamburg, Missionary in Denmark and Sweden, 865** Ordinary Time starts today (or on 2 February if The Presentation is observed on 1 February)			
Gw	Com. Missionary *esp.* Isa. 52. 7–10 *also* Rom. 10. 11–15	*or* 2 Sam. 18.9–10, 14, 24–25, 30 – 19.3 Ps. 86. 1–6 Mark 5. 21–end	Ps. ***5***; 6; (8) Gen. 18. 16–end Matt. 27. 27–44	Ps. ***9***; 10† Hos. ch. 10 1 Cor. ch. 13

4 Wednesday	*Gilbert of Sempringham, Founder of the Gilbertine Order, 1189*			
G		2 Sam. 24. 2, 9–17 Ps. 32. 1–8 Mark 6. 1–6a	Ps. 119. 1–32 Gen. 19. 1–3, 12–29 Matt. 27. 45–56	Ps. ***11***; 12; 13 Hos. 11. 1–11 1 Cor. 14. 1–19

*See provision for First EP on 1 February and throughout the day for The Presentation on 2 February.

		Sunday Principal Service Weekday Eucharist	Third Service Morning Prayer	Second Service Evening Prayer
5 Thursday				
G		1 Kings 2. 1–4, 10–12 *Canticle*: 1 Chron. 29. 10–12 *or* Ps. 145. 1–5 Mark 6. 7–13	Ps. 14; ***15***; 16 Gen. 21. 1–21 Matt. 27. 57–end	Ps. 18† Hos. 11.12 – 12.end 1 Cor. 14. 20–end
6 Friday	*The Martyrs of Japan, 1597*			
G		Ecclus. 47. 2–11 Ps. 18. 31–36, 50–end Mark 6. 14–29	Ps. 17; ***19*** Gen. 22. 1–19 Matt. 28. 1–15	Ps. 22 Hos. 13. 1–14 1 Cor. 16. 1–9
7 Saturday				
G		1 Kings 3. 4–13 Ps. 119. 9–16 Mark 6. 30–34	Ps. 20; 21; ***23*** Gen. ch. 23 Matt. 28. 16–end	Ps. ***24***; 25 Hos. ch. 14 1 Cor. 16. 10–end **ct**

8 Sunday	**THE SECOND SUNDAY BEFORE LENT**		
G	Gen. 1.1 – 2.3 Ps. 136 (*or* 136. 1–9, 23–end) Rom. 8. 18–25 Matt. 6. 25–end	Ps. 100; 150 Job 38. 1–21 Col. 1. 15–20	Ps. 148 Prov. 8. 1, 22–31 Rev. ch. 4 *Gospel*: Luke 12. 16–31
9 Monday			
G **DEL 5**	1 Kings 8. 1–7, 9–13 Ps. 132. 1–9 Mark 6. 53–end	Ps. 27; ***30*** Gen. 29.31 – 30.24 2 Tim. 4. 1–8	Ps. 26; ***28***; 29 2 Chron. 9. 1–12 John 19. 1–16
10 Tuesday	*Scholastica, sister of Benedict, Abbess of Plombariola, c. 543*		
G	1 Kings 8. 22–23, 27–30 Ps. 84. 1–10 Mark 7. 1–13	Ps. 32; ***36*** Gen. 31. 1–24 2 Tim. 4. 9–end	Ps. 33 2 Chron. 10.1 – 11.4 John 19. 17–30
11 Wednesday			
G	1 Kings 10. 1–10 Ps. 37. 3–6, 30–32 Mark 7. 14–23	Ps. 34 Gen. 31.25 – 32.2 Titus ch. 1	Ps. 119. 33–56 2 Chron. ch. 12 John 19. 31–end

		Sunday Principal Service Weekday Eucharist	Third Service Morning Prayer	Second Service Evening Prayer
12 Thursday				
G		1 Kings 11. 4–13 Ps. 106. 3, 35–41 Mark 7. 24–30	Ps. 37† Gen. 32. 3–30 Titus ch. 2	Ps. 39; ***40*** 2 Chron. 13.1 – 14.1 John 20. 1–10
13 Friday				
G		1 Kings 11. 29–32; 12. 19 Ps. 81. 8–14 Mark 7. 31–end	Ps. 31 Gen. 33. 1–17 Titus ch. 3	Ps. 35 2 Chron. 14. 2–end John 20. 11–18
14 Saturday	**Cyril and Methodius, Missionaries to the Slavs, 869 and 885** *Valentine, Martyr at Rome, c. 269*			
Gw	Com. Missionaries *esp.* Isa. 52. 7–10 *also* Rom. 10. 11–15	*or* 1 Kings 12. 26–32; 13. 33–end Ps. 106. 6–7, 20–23 Mark 8. 1–10	Ps. 41; ***42***; 43 Gen. ch. 35 Philemon	Ps. 45; ***46*** 2 Chron. 15. 1–15 John 20. 19–end **ct**

15 Sunday	**THE SUNDAY NEXT BEFORE LENT**				
G			Exod. 24. 12–end Ps. 2 *or* Ps. 99 2 Pet. 1. 16–end Matt. 17. 1–9	Ps. 72 Exod. 34. 29–end 2 Cor. 4. 3–6	Ps. 84 Ecclus. 48. 1–10 *or* 2 Kings 2. 1–12 Matt. 17. 9–23 (*or* 1–23)
16 Monday					
G **DEL 6**			James 1. 1–11 Ps. 119. 65–72 Mark 8. 11–13	Ps. 44 Gen. 37. 1–11 Gal. ch. 1	Ps. ***47***; 49 Jer. ch. 1 John 3. 1–21
17 Tuesday	**Janani Luwum, Archbishop of Uganda, Martyr, 1977**				
Gr	Com. Martyr *also* Ecclus. 4. 20–28 John 12. 24–32	*or*	James 1. 12–18 Ps. 94. 12–18 Mark 8. 14–21	Ps. ***48***; 52 Gen. 37. 12–end Gal. 2. 1–10	Ps. 50 Jer. 2. 1–13 John 3. 22–end

		Sunday Principal Service Weekday Eucharist	Third Service Morning Prayer	Second Service Evening Prayer
18 Wednesday	**ASH WEDNESDAY**			
P		Joel 2. 1–2, 12–17 *or* Isa. 58. 1–12 Ps. 51. 1–18 2 Cor. 5.20b - 6.10 Matt. 6. 1–6, 16–21 *or* John 8. 1–11	*MP*: Ps. 38 Dan. 9. 3–6, 17–19 1 Tim. 6. 6–19	*EP*: Ps. ***51*** *or* Ps. 102 (*or* 102.1–18) Isa. 1. 10–18 Luke 15. 11–end
19 Thursday				
P		Deut. 30. 15–end Ps. 1 Luke 9. 22–25	Ps. 77 *alt*. Ps. 56; ***57***; (63†) Gen. ch. 39 Gal. 2. 11–end	Ps. 74 *alt*. Ps. 61; ***62***; 64 Jer. 2. 14–32 John 4. 1–26
20 Friday				
P		Isa. 58. 1–9a Ps. 51. 1–5, 17–18 Matt. 9. 14–15	Ps. ***3***; 7 *alt*. Ps. ***51***; 54 Gen. ch. 40 Gal. 3. 1–14	Ps. 31 *alt*. Ps. 38 Jer. 3. 6–22 John 4. 27–42

21 Saturday					
P			Isa. 58. 9b–end Ps. 86. 1–7 Luke 5. 27–32	Ps. 71 *alt.* Ps. 68 Gen. 41. 1–24 Gal. 3. 15–22	Ps. 73 *alt.* Ps. 65; ***66*** Jer. 4. 1–18 John 4. 43–end **ct**
22 Sunday	**THE FIRST SUNDAY OF LENT**				
P			Gen. 2. 15–17; 3. 1–7 Ps. 32 Rom. 5. 12–19 Matt. 4. 1–11	Ps. 119. 1–16 Jer. 18. 1–11 Luke 18. 9–14	Ps. 50. 1–15 Deut. 6. 4–9, 16–end Luke 15. 1–10
23 Monday	**Polycarp, Bishop of Smyrna, Martyr, c. 155**				
Pr	Com. Martyr *also* Rev. 2. 8–11	*or*	Lev. 19. 1–2, 11–18 Ps. 19. 7–end Matt. 25. 31–end	Ps. 10; ***11*** *alt.* Ps. 71 Gen. 41. 25–45 Gal. 3.23 – 4.7	Ps. 12; ***13***; 14 *alt.* Ps. ***72***; 75 Jer. 4. 19–end John 5. 1–18

February/ March 2026		Sunday Principal Service Weekday Eucharist	Third Service Morning Prayer	Second Service Evening Prayer
24 Tuesday*				
P		Isa. 55. 10–11 Ps. 34. 4–6, 21–22 Matt. 6. 7–15	Ps. 44 *alt.* Ps. 73 Gen. 41.46 - 42.5 Gal. 4. 8–20	Ps. 46; ***49*** *alt.* Ps. 74 Jer. 5. 1–19 John 5. 19–29
25 Wednesday	Ember Day			
P		Jonah ch. 3 Ps. 51. 1–5, 17–18 Luke 11. 29–32	Ps. ***6***; 17 *alt.* Ps. 77 Gen. 42. 6–17 Gal. 4.21 - 5.1	Ps. 9; ***28*** *alt.* Ps. 119. 81–104 Jer. 5. 20–end John 5. 30–end
26 Thursday				
P		Esther 14. 1–5, 12–14 *or* Isa. 55. 6–9 Ps. 138 Matt. 7. 7–12	Ps. ***42***; 43 *alt.* Ps. 78. 1–39† Gen. 42. 18–28 Gal. 5. 2–15	Ps. 137; 138; ***142*** *alt.* Ps. 78. 40–end† Jer. 6. 9–21 John 6. 1–15

27 Friday	**George Herbert, Priest, Poet, 1633** Ember Day			
Pw	Com. Pastor *esp.* Mal. 2. 5–7 Matt. 11. 25–end *also* Rev. 19. 5–9	*or* Ezek. 18. 21–28 Ps. 130 Matt. 5. 20–26	Ps. 22 *alt.* Ps. 55 Gen. 42. 29–end Gal. 5. 16–end	Ps. 54; ***55*** *alt.* Ps. 69 Jer. 6. 22–end John 6. 16–27
28 Saturday	Ember Day			
P		Deut. 26. 16–end Ps. 119. 1–8 Matt. 5. 43–end	Ps. 59; ***63*** *alt.* Ps. ***76***; 79 Gen. 43. 1–15 Gal. ch. 6	Ps. ***4***; 16 *alt.* Ps. 81; ***84*** Jer. 7. 1–20 John 6. 27–40 **ct**

March 2026

1 Sunday	**THE SECOND SUNDAY OF LENT**			
P		Gen. 12. 1–4a Ps. 121 Rom. 4. 1–5, 13–17 John 3. 1–17	Ps. 74 Jer. 22. 1–9 Matt. 8. 1–13	Ps. 135 (*or* 135. 1–14) Num. 21. 4–9 Luke 14. 27–33

*Matthias may be celebrated on 24 February instead of 15 May.

March 2026		Sunday Principal Service Weekday Eucharist	Third Service Morning Prayer	Second Service Evening Prayer
2 Monday	**Chad, Bishop of Lichfield, Missionary, 672***			
Pw	Com. Missionary *or* *also* 1 Tim. 6. 11b-16	Dan. 9. 4-10 Ps. 79. 8-9, 12, 14 Luke 6. 36-38	Ps. 26; ***32*** *alt*. Ps. ***80***; 82 Gen. 43. 16-end Heb. ch. 1	Ps. 70; ***74*** *alt*. Ps. ***85***; 86 Jer. 7. 21-end John 6. 41-51
3 Tuesday				
P		Isa. 1. 10, 16-20 Ps. 50. 8, 16-end Matt. 23. 1-12	Ps. 50 *alt*. Ps. 87; ***89. 1-18*** Gen. 44. 1-17 Heb. 2. 1-9	Ps. ***52***; 53; 54 *alt*. Ps. 89. 19-end Jer. 8. 1-15 John 6. 52-59
4 Wednesday				
P		Jer. 18. 18-20 Ps. 31. 4-5, 14-18 Matt. 20. 17-28	Ps. 35 *alt*. Ps. 119. 105-128 Gen. 44. 18-end Heb. 2. 10-end	Ps. ***3***; 51 *alt*. Ps. ***91***; 93 Jer. 8.18 - 9.11 John 6. 60-end

5 Thursday					
P			Jer. 17. 5–10 Ps. 1 Luke 16. 19–end	Ps. 34 *alt.* Ps. 90; **92** Gen. 45. 1–15 Heb. 3. 1–6	Ps. 71 *alt.* Ps. 94 Jer. 9. 12–24 John 7. 1–13
6 Friday					
P			Gen. 37. 3–4, 12–13, 17–28 Ps. 105. 16–22 Matt. 21. 33–43, 45–46	Ps. 40; ***41*** *alt.* Ps. ***88***; (95) Gen. 45. 16–end Heb. 3. 7–end	Ps. ***6***; 38 *alt.* Ps. 102 Jer. 10. 1–16 John 7. 14–24
7 Saturday	**Perpetua, Felicity and their Companions, Martyrs at Carthage, 203**				
Pr	Com. Martyr *esp.* Rev. 12. 10–12a *also* Wisd. 3. 1–7	*or*	Mic. 7. 14–15, 18–20 Ps. 103. 1–4, 9–12 Luke 15. 1–3, 11–end	Ps. 3; ***25*** *alt.* Ps. 96; ***97***; 100 Gen. 46. 1–7, 28–end Heb. 4. 1–13	Ps. ***23***; 27 *alt.* Ps. 104 Jer. 10. 17–24 John 7. 25–36 **ct**

*Chad may be celebrated with Cedd on 26 October instead of 2 March.

March 2026		Sunday Principal Service Weekday Eucharist	Third Service Morning Prayer	Second Service Evening Prayer
8 Sunday	**THE THIRD SUNDAY OF LENT**			
P		Exod. 17. 1–7 Ps. 95 Rom. 5. 1–11 John 4. 5–42	Ps. 46 Amos 7. 10–end 2 Cor. 1. 1–11	Ps. 40 Josh. 1. 1–9 Eph. 6. 10–20 *Gospel*: John 2. 13–22
9 Monday*				
P		2 Kings 5. 1–15 Ps. 42. 1–2; 43. 1–4 Luke 4. 24–30	Ps. ***5***; 7 *alt.* Ps. ***98***; 99; 101 Gen. 47. 1–27 Heb. 4.14 – 5.10	Ps. 11; ***17*** *alt.* Ps. ***105***† (*or* 103) Jer. 11. 1–17 John 7. 37–52
10 Tuesday				
P		Song of the Three 2, 11–20 *or* Dan. 2. 20–23 Ps. 25. 3–10 Matt. 18. 21–end	Ps. 6; ***9*** *alt.* Ps. ***106***† (*or* 103) Gen. 47.28 – 48.end Heb. 5.11 – 6.12	Ps. 61; 62; ***64*** *alt.* Ps. 107† Jer. 11.18 – 12.6 John 7.53 – 8.11

11 Wednesday

P	Deut. 4. 1, 5–9 Ps. 147. 13–end Matt. 5. 17–19	Ps. 38 *alt.* Ps. 110; ***111***; 112 Gen. 49. 1–32 Heb. 6. 13–end	Ps. 36; ***39*** *alt.* Ps. 119. 129–152 Jer. 13. 1–11 John 8. 12–30

12 Thursday

P	Jer. 7. 23–28 Ps. 95. 1–2, 6–end Luke 11. 14–23	Ps. ***56***; 57 *alt.* Ps. 113; ***115*** Gen. 49.33 – 50.end Heb. 7. 1–10	Ps. ***59***; 60 *alt.* Ps. 114; ***116***; 117 Jer. ch. 14 John 8. 31–47

13 Friday

P	Hos. ch. 14 Ps. 81. 6–10, 13, 16 Mark 12. 28–34	Ps. 22 *alt.* Ps. 139 Exod. 1. 1–14 Heb. 7. 11–end	Ps. 69 *alt.* Ps. ***130***; 131; 137 Jer. 15. 10–end John 8. 48–end

*The following readings may replace those provided for Holy Communion on any day during the Third Week of Lent: Exod. 17. 1–7; Ps. 95. 1–2, 6–end; John 4. 5–42.

		Sunday Principal Service Weekday Eucharist	Third Service Morning Prayer	Second Service Evening Prayer
14 Saturday				
P		Hos. 5.15 – 6.6 Ps. 51. 1–2, 17–end Luke 18. 9–14	Ps. 31 *alt.* Ps. 120; ***121***; 122 Exod. 1.22 – 2.10 Heb. ch. 8	Ps. ***116***; 130 *alt.* Ps. 118 Jer. 16.10 – 17.4 John 9. 1–17 **ct**
15 Sunday	**THE FOURTH SUNDAY OF LENT** (Mothering Sunday)			
P		1 Sam. 16. 1–13 Ps. 23 Eph. 5. 8–14 John ch. 9	Ps. 19 Isa. 43. 1–7 Eph. 2. 8–14	Ps. 31. 1–16 (*or* 31. 1–8) Mic. ch. 7 *or* Prayer of Manasseh James ch. 5 *Gospel*: John 3. 14–21 *If the Principal Service readings for The Fourth Sunday of Lent are displaced by Mothering Sunday provisions, they may be used at the Second Service.*

or, for Mothering Sunday:

Exod. 2. 1–10
or 1 Sam. 1. 20–end
Ps. 34. 11–20
or Ps. 127. 1–4
2 Cor. 1. 3–7
or Col. 3. 12–17
Luke 2. 33–35
or John 19. 25b–27

16 Monday*

P		Isa. 65. 17–21 Ps. 30. 1–5, 8, 11–end John 4. 43–end	Ps. 70; ***77*** *alt.* Ps. 123; 124; 125; ***126*** Exod. 2. 11–22 Heb. 9. 1–14	Ps. ***25***; 28 *alt.* Ps. ***127***; 128; 129 Jer. 17. 5–18 John 9. 18–end

17 Tuesday **Patrick, Bishop, Missionary, Patron of Ireland, c. 460**

Pw	Com. Missionary *also* Ps. 91. 1–4, 13–end Luke 10. 1–12, 17–20	*or* Ezek. 47. 1–9, 12 Ps. 46. 1–8 John 5. 1–3, 5–16	Ps. 54; ***79*** *alt.* Ps. ***132***; 133 Exod. 2.23 – 3.20 Heb. 9. 15–end	Ps. ***80***; 82 *alt.* Ps. (134); ***135*** Jer. 18. 1–12 John 10. 1–10

*The following readings may replace those provided for Holy Communion on any day (except St Joseph's Day) during the Fourth Week of Lent: Mic. 7. 7–9; Ps. 27. 1, 9–10, 16–17; John ch. 9.

March 2026		Sunday Principal Service Weekday Eucharist	Third Service Morning Prayer	Second Service Evening Prayer
18 Wednesday	*Cyril, Bishop of Jerusalem, Teacher, 386*			
P		Isa. 49. 8–15 Ps. 145. 8–18 John 5. 17–30	Ps. 63; ***90*** *alt.* Ps. 119. 153–end Exod. 4. 1–23 Heb. 10. 1–18	Ps. 52; ***91*** *alt.* Ps. 136 Jer. 18. 13–end John 10. 11–21 *or First EP of Joseph* Ps. 132 Hos. 11. 1–9 Luke 2. 41–end **W ct**
19 Thursday	**JOSEPH OF NAZARETH**			
W		2 Sam. 7. 4–16 Ps. 89. 26–36 Rom. 4. 13–18 Matt. 1. 18–end	*MP*: Ps. 25; 147. 1–12 Isa. 11. 1–10 Matt. 13. 54–end	*EP*: Ps. 1; 112 Gen. 50. 22–end Matt. 2. 13–end
20 Friday	**Cuthbert, Bishop of Lindisfarne, Missionary, 687***			
Pw	Com. Missionary *esp.* Ezek. 34. 11–16 *also* Matt. 18. 12–14 *or*	Wisd. 2. 1, 12–22 *or* Jer. 26. 8–11 Ps. 34. 15–end John 7. 1–2, 10, 25–30	Ps. 102 *alt.* Ps. 142; ***144*** Exod. 6. 2–13 Heb. 10. 26–end	Ps. 13; ***16*** *alt.* Ps. 145 Jer. 19.14 – 20.6 John 11. 1–16

21 Saturday	**Thomas Cranmer, Archbishop of Canterbury, Reformation Martyr, 1556**				
Pr	Com. Martyr	*or*	Jer. 11. 18–20 Ps. 7. 1–2, 8–10 John 7. 40–52	Ps. 32 *alt.* Ps. 147 Exod. 7. 8–end Heb. 11. 1–16	Ps. ***140***; 141; 142 *alt.* Ps. ***148***; 149; 150 Jer. 20. 7–end John 11. 17–27 **ct**
22 Sunday	THE FIFTH SUNDAY OF LENT (Passiontide begins)				
P			Ezek. 37. 1–14 Ps. 130 Rom. 8. 6–11 John 11. 1–45	Ps. 86 Jer. 31. 27–37 John 12. 20–33	Ps. 30 Lam. 3. 19–33 Matt. 20. 17–end
23 Monday**					
P			Susanna 1–9, 15–17, 19–30, 33–62 (*or* 41b–62) *or* Josh. 2. 1–14 Ps. 23 John 8. 1–11	Ps. ***73***; 121 *alt.* Ps. ***1***; 2; 3 Exod. 8. 1–19 Heb. 11. 17–31	Ps. ***26***; 27 *alt.* Ps. ***4***; 7 Jer. 21. 1–10 John 11. 28–44

*Cuthbert may be celebrated on 4 September instead of 20 March.

**The following readings may replace those provided for Holy Communion on any day (except The Annunciation) during the Fifth Week of Lent: 2 Kings 4. 18–21, 32–37; Ps. 17. 1–8, 16; John 11. 1–45.

		Sunday Principal Service Weekday Eucharist	Third Service Morning Prayer	Second Service Evening Prayer
24 Tuesday	*Walter Hilton of Thurgarton, Augustinian Canon, Mystic, 1396; Paul Couturier, Priest, Ecumenist, 1953; Oscar Romero, Archbishop of San Salvador, Martyr, 1980*			
P		Num. 21. 4–9 Ps. 102. 1–3, 16–23 John 8. 21–30	Ps. ***35***; 123 *alt.* Ps. ***5***; 6; (8) Exod. 8. 20–end Heb. 11.32 – 12.2	*First EP of The Annunciation* Ps. 85 Wisd. 9. 1–12 *or* Gen. 3. 8–15 Gal. 4. 1–5 **𝔚 ct**
25 Wednesday	**THE ANNUNCIATION OF OUR LORD TO THE BLESSED VIRGIN MARY**			
𝔚		Isa. 7. 10–14 Ps. 40. 5–11 Heb. 10. 4–10 Luke 1. 26–38	*MP*: Ps. 111; 113 1 Sam. 2. 1–10 Rom. 5. 12–end	*EP*: Ps. 131; 146 Isa. 52. 1–12 Heb. 2. 5–end
26 Thursday	*Harriet Monsell, Founder of the Community of St John the Baptist, Clewer, 1883*			
P		Gen. 17. 3–9 Ps. 105. 4–9 John 8. 51–end	Ps. ***40***; 125 *alt.* Ps. 14; ***15***; 16 Exod. 9. 13–end Heb. 12. 14–end	Ps. 42; ***43*** *alt.* Ps. 18† Jer. 23. 9–32 John 12. 12–19

27 Friday				
P		Jer. 20. 10–13 Ps. 18. 1–6 John 10. 31–end	Ps. ***22***; 126 *alt.* Ps. 17; ***19*** Exod. ch. 10 Heb. 13. 1–16	Ps. 31 *alt.* Ps. 22 Jer. ch. 24 John 12. 20–36a
28 Saturday				
P		Ezek. 37. 21–end *Canticle*: Jer. 31. 10–13 *or* Ps. 121 John 11. 45–end	Ps. ***23***; 127 *alt.* Ps. 20; 21; ***23*** Exod. ch. 11 Heb. 13. 17–end	Ps. 128; 129; ***130*** *alt.* Ps. ***24***; 25 Jer. 25. 1–14 John 12. 36b–end **ct**
29 Sunday	**PALM SUNDAY**			
R	*Liturgy of the Palms* Matt. 21. 1–11 Ps. 118. 1–2, 19–end (*or* 118. 19–24)	*Liturgy of the Passion* Isa. 50. 4–9a Ps. 31. 9–16 (*or* 31. 9–18) Phil. 2. 5–11 Matt. 26.14 – 27.end *or* Matt. 27. 11–54	Ps. 61; 62 Zech. 9. 9–12 Luke 16. 19–end	Ps. 80 Isa. 5. 1–7 Matt. 21. 33–end

		Sunday Principal Service Weekday Eucharist	Third Service Morning Prayer	Second Service Evening Prayer
30 Monday	**MONDAY OF HOLY WEEK**			
R		Isa. 42. 1–9 Ps. 36. 5–11 Heb. 9. 11–15 John 12. 1–11	*MP*: Ps. 41 Lam. 1. 1–12a Luke 22. 1–23	*EP*: Ps. 25 Lam. 2. 8–19 Col. 1. 18–23
31 Tuesday	**TUESDAY OF HOLY WEEK**			
R		Isa. 49. 1–7 Ps. 71. 1–14 (*or* 71. 1–8) 1 Cor. 1. 18–31 John 12. 20–36	*MP*: Ps. 27 Lam. 3. 1–18 Luke 22. [24–38] 39–53	*EP*: Ps. 55. 13–24 Lam. 3. 40–51 Gal. 6. 11–end

April 2026

1 Wednesday	**WEDNESDAY OF HOLY WEEK**			
R		Isa. 50. 4–9a Ps. 70 Heb. 12. 1–3 John 13. 21–32	*MP*: Ps. 102 (*or* 102. 1–18) Wisd. 1.16 – 2.1, 12–22 *or* Jer. 11. 18–20 Luke 22. 54–end	*EP*: Ps. 88 Isa. 63. 1–9 Rev. 14.18 – 15.4

2 Thursday	**MAUNDY THURSDAY**			
W(HC)R		Exod. 12. 1–14 (*or* 12. 1–4, 11–14) Ps. 116. 1, 10–end (*or* 116. 9–end) 1 Cor. 11. 23–26 John 13. 1–17, 31b–35	*MP*: Ps. 42; 43 Lev. 16. 2–24 Luke 23. 1–25	*EP*: Ps. 39 Exod. ch. 11 Eph. 2. 11–18
3 Friday	**GOOD FRIDAY**			
R		Isa. 52.13 – 53.end Ps. 22 (*or* 22. 1–11 *or* 22. 1–21) Heb. 10. 16–25 *or* Heb. 4. 14–16; 5. 7–9 John 18.1 – 19.end	*MP*: Ps. 69 Gen. 22. 1–18 A part of John 18 – 19 if not read at the Principal Service *or* Heb. 10. 1–10	*EP*: Ps. 130; 143 Lam. 5. 15–end A part of John 18 – 19 if not read at the Principal Service, esp. John 19. 38–end *or* Col. 1. 18–23
4 Saturday	**EASTER EVE**			
	These readings are for use at services other than the Easter Vigil	Job 14. 1–14 *or* Lam. 3. 1–9, 19–24 Ps. 31. 1–4, 15–16 (*or* 31. 1–5) 1 Pet. 4. 1–8 Matt. 27. 57–end *or* John 19. 38–end	Ps. 142 Hos. 6. 1–6 John 2. 18–22	Ps. 116 Job 19. 21–27 1 John 5. 5–12

April 2026		Sunday Principal Service Weekday Eucharist	Third Service Morning Prayer	Second Service Evening Prayer
5 Sunday	**EASTER DAY**			
𝔚	*The following readings and psalms (or canticles) are provided for use at the Easter Vigil. A minimum of three Old Testament readings should be chosen. The reading from* Exodus ch. 14 *should always be used.*	Gen. 1.1 - 2.4a & Ps. 136. 1–9, 23–end Gen. 7. 1–5, 11–18; 8. 6–18; 9. 8–13 & Ps. 46 Gen. 22. 1–18 & Ps. 16 Exod. 14. 10–end; 15. 20–21 & *Canticle*: Exod. 15. 1b–13, 17–18 Isa. 55. 1–11 & *Canticle*: Isa. 12. 2–end Baruch 3.9–15, 32 - 4.4 & Ps. 19 *or* Prov. 8. 1–8, 19–21; 9. 4b–6 & Ps. 19 Ezek. 36. 24–28 & Ps. 42; 43 Ezek. 37. 1–14 & Ps. 143 Zeph. 3. 14–end & Ps. 98 Rom. 6. 3–11 & Ps. 114 Matt. 28. 1–10		
𝔚	*Easter Day Services* *The reading from Acts must be used as either the first or second reading at the Principal Service.*	Acts 10. 34–43 *or* Jer. 31. 1–6 Ps. 118. 1–2, 14–24 (*or* 118. 14–24) Col. 3. 1–4 *or* Acts 10. 34–43 John 20. 1–18 *or* Matt. 28. 1–10	*MP*: Ps. 114; 117 Exod. 14.10–18, 26 - 15.2 Rev. 15. 2–4	*EP*: Ps. 105 *or* Ps. 66. 1–11 Song of Sol. 3. 2–5; 8. 6–7 John 20. 11–18 *if not used at the Principal Service* *or* Rev. 1. 12–18

6 Monday **MONDAY OF EASTER WEEK**

W	Acts 2. 14, 22–32 Ps. 16. 1–2, 6–end Matt. 28. 8–15	Ps. ***111***; 117; 146 Exod. 12. 1–14 1 Cor. 15. 1–11	Ps. 135 Song of Sol. 1.9 – 2.7 Mark 16. 1–8

7 Tuesday **TUESDAY OF EASTER WEEK**

W	Acts 2. 36–41 Ps. 33. 4–5, 18–end John 20. 11–18	Ps. ***112***; 147. 1–12 Exod. 12. 14–36 1 Cor. 15. 12–19	Ps. 136 Song of Sol. 2. 8–end Luke 24. 1–12

8 Wednesday **WEDNESDAY OF EASTER WEEK**

W	Acts 3. 1–10 Ps. 105. 1–9 Luke 24. 13–35	Ps. ***113***; 147. 13–end Exod. 12. 37–end 1 Cor. 15. 20–28	Ps. 105 Song of Sol. ch. 3 Matt. 28. 16–end

9 Thursday **THURSDAY OF EASTER WEEK**

W	Acts 3. 11–end Ps. 8 Luke 24. 35–48	Ps. ***114***; 148 Exod. 13. 1–16 1 Cor. 15. 29–34	Ps. 106 Song of Sol. 5.2 – 6.3 Luke 7. 11–17

		Sunday Principal Service Weekday Eucharist	Third Service Morning Prayer	Second Service Evening Prayer
10 Friday	**FRIDAY OF EASTER WEEK**			
W		Acts 4. 1–12 Ps. 118. 1–4, 22–26 John 21. 1–14	Ps. ***115***; 149 Exod. 13.17 – 14.14 1 Cor. 15. 35-50	Ps. 107 Song of Sol. 7.10 – 8.4 Luke 8. 41–end
11 Saturday	**SATURDAY OF EASTER WEEK**			
W		Acts 4. 13–21 Ps. 118. 1–4, 14–21 Mark 16. 9–15	Ps. ***116***; 150 Exod. 14. 15–end 1 Cor. 15. 51–end	Ps. 145 Song of Sol. 8. 5–7 John 11. 17–44 **ct**
12 Sunday	**THE SECOND SUNDAY OF EASTER**			
W	*The reading from Acts must be used as either the first or second reading at the Principal Service.*	Acts 2. 14a, 22–32 [or Exod. 14. 10–end; 15. 20–21] Ps. 16 1 Pet. 1. 3–9 John 20. 19–end	Ps. 81. 1–10 Exod. 12. 1–17 1 Cor. 5. 6b–8	Ps. 30. 1–5 Dan. 6. 1–23 (*or* 6. 6–23) Mark 15.46 – 16.8

13 Monday

W	Acts 4. 23–31 Ps. 2. 1–9 John 3. 1–8	Ps. 2; ***19*** *alt.* Ps. ***1***; 2; 3 Exod. 15. 1–21 Col. 1. 1–14	Ps. 139 *alt.* Ps. ***4***; 7 Deut. 1. 3–18 John 20. 1–10

14 Tuesday

W	Acts 4. 32–end Ps. 93 John 3. 7–15	Ps. ***8***; 20; 21 *alt.* Ps. ***5***; 6; (8) Exod. 15.22 – 16.10 Col. 1. 15–end	Ps. 104 *alt.* Ps. 9; ***10***† Deut. 1. 19–40 John 20. 11–18

15 Wednesday

W	Acts 5. 17–26 Ps. 34. 1–8 John 3. 16–21	Ps. 16; ***30*** *alt.* Ps. 119. 1–32 Exod. 16. 11–end Col. 2. 1–15	Ps. 33 *alt.* Ps. ***11***; 12; 13 Deut. 3. 18–end John 20. 19–end

16 Thursday *Isabella Gilmcre, Deconess, 1923*

W	Acts 5. 27–33 Ps. 34. 1, 15–end John 3. 31–end	Ps. ***28***; 29 *alt.* Ps. 14; ***15***; 16 Exod. ch. 17 Col. 2.16 – 3.11	Ps. 34 *alt.* Ps. 18† Deut. 4. 1–14 John 21. 1–14

April 2026		Sunday Principal Service Weekday Eucharist	Third Service Morning Prayer	Second Service Evening Prayer
17 Friday				
W		Acts 5. 34–42 Ps. 27. 1–5, 16–17 John 6. 1–15	Ps. 57; ***61*** *alt.* Ps. 17; ***19*** Exod. 18. 1–12 Col. 3.12 – 4.1	Ps. 118 *alt.* Ps. 22 Deut. 4. 15–31 John 21. 15–19
18 Saturday				
W		Acts 6. 1–7 Ps. 33. 1–5, 18–19 John 6. 16–21	Ps. 63; ***84*** *alt.* Ps. 20; 21; **23** Exod. 18. 13–end Col. 4. 2–end	Ps. 66 *alt.* Ps. ***24***; 25 Deut. 4. 32–40 John 21. 20–end **ct**
19 Sunday	**THE THIRD SUNDAY OF EASTER**			
W	*The reading from Acts must be used as either the first or second reading at the Principal Service.*	Acts 2. 14a, 36–41 [or Zeph. 3. 14–end] Ps. 116. 1–3, 10–end (or 116. 1–7) 1 Pet. 1. 17–23 Luke 24. 13–35	Ps. 23 Isa. 40. 1–11 1 Pet. 5. 1–11	Ps. 48 Hag. 1.13 – 2.9 1 Cor. 3. 10–17 *Gospel*: John 2. 13–22

20 Monday					
W			Acts 6. 8–15 Ps. 119. 17–24 John 6. 22–29	Ps. ***96***; 97 *alt*. Ps. 27; ***30*** Exod. ch. 19 Luke 1. 1–25	Ps. ***61***; 65 *alt*. Ps. 26; ***28***; 29 Deut. 5. 1–22 Eph. 1. 1–14
21 Tuesday	**Anselm, Abbot of Le Bec, Archbishop of Canterbury, Teacher, 1109**				
W	Com. Teacher *also* Wisd. 9. 13-end Rom. 5. 8–11	*or*	Acts 7.51 – 8.1a Ps. 31. 1–5, 16 John 6. 30–35	Ps. ***98***; 99; 100 *alt*. Ps. 32; ***36*** Exod. 20. 1–21 Luke 1. 26–38	Ps. 71 *alt*. Ps. 33 Deut. 5. 22–end Eph. 1. 15–end
22 Wednesday					
W			Acts 8. 1b–8 Ps. 66. 1–6 John 6. 35–40	Ps. 105 *alt*. Ps. 34 Exod. ch. 24 Luke 1. 39–56	Ps. 67; ***72*** *alt*. Ps. 119. 33–56 Deut. ch. 6 Eph. 2. 1–10 *or First EP of George* Ps. 111; 116 Jer. 15. 15–end Heb. 11.32 – 12.2 **R ct**

		Sunday Principal Service Weekday Eucharist	Third Service Morning Prayer	Second Service Evening Prayer
23 Thursday	**GEORGE, MARTYR, PATRON OF ENGLAND, c. 304**			
R		1 Macc. 2. 59–64 *or* Rev. 12. 7–12 Ps. 126 2 Tim. 2. 3–13 John 15. 18–21	*MP*: Ps. 5; 146 Josh. 1. 1–9 Eph. 6. 10–20	*EP*: Ps. 3; 11 Isa. 43. 1–7 John 15. 1–8
24 Friday	*Mellitus, Bishop of London, first Bishop at St Paul's, 624; The Seven Martyrs of the Melanesian Brotherhood, Solomon Islands, 2003*			
W		Acts 9. 1–20 Ps. 117 John 6. 52–59	Ps. 107 *alt.* Ps. 31 Exod. 28. 1–4a, 29–38 Luke 2. 1–20	Ps. 77 *alt.* Ps. 35 Deut. 7. 12–end Eph. 3. 1–13 *or First EP of Mark*: Ps. 19 Isa. 52. 7–10 Mark 1. 1–15 **R ct**

25 Saturday	**MARK THE EVANGELIST**			
R		Prov. 15. 28–end *or* Acts 15. 35–end Ps. 119. 9–16 Eph. 4. 7–16 Mark 13. 5–13	*MP*: Ps. 37. 23–end; 148 Isa. 62. 6–10 *or* Ecclus. 51. 13–end Acts 12.25 - 13.13	*EP*: Ps. 45 Ezek. 1. 4–14 2 Tim. 4. 1–11
26 Sunday	**THE FOURTH SUNDAY OF EASTER**			
W	*The reading from Acts must be used as either the first or second reading at the Principal Service.*	Acts 2. 42–end [*or* Gen. ch. 7] Ps. 23 1 Pet. 2. 19–end John 10. 1–10	Ps. 106. 6–24 Neh. 9. 6–15 1 Cor. 10. 1–13	Ps. 29. 1–10 Ezra 3. 1–13 Eph. 2. 11–end *Gospel*: Luke 19. 37–end
27 Monday	*Christina Rossetti, Poet, 1894*			
W		Acts 11. 1–18 Ps. 42. 1–2; 43. 1–4 John 10. 1–10 (*or* 11–18)	Ps. 103 *alt.* Ps. 44 Exod. 32. 1–14 Luke 2. 41–end	Ps. 112; 113; ***114*** *alt.* Ps. ***47***; 49 Deut. 9. 1–21 Eph. 4. 1–16

April/May 2026		Sunday Principal Service Weekday Eucharist	Third Service Morning Prayer	Second Service Evening Prayer
28 Tuesday	*Peter Chanel, Missionary in the South Pacific, Martyr, 1841*			
W		Acts 11. 19–26 Ps. 87 John 10. 22–30	Ps. 139 *alt.* Ps. ***48***; 52 Exod. 32. 15–34 Luke 3. 1–14	Ps. 116; ***116*** *alt.* Ps. 50 Deut. 9.23 – 10.5 Eph. 4. 17–end
29 Wednesday	**Catherine of Siena, Teacher, 1380**			
W	Com. Teacher *also* Prov. 8. 1, 6–11 John 17. 12–26	*or* Acts 12.24 – 13.5 Ps. 67 John 12. 44–end	Ps. 135 *alt.* Ps. 119. 57–80 Exod. ch. 33 Luke 3. 15–22	Ps. ***47***; 48 *alt.* Ps. ***59***; 60 (67) Deut. 10. 12–end Eph. 5. 1–14
30 Thursday	*Pandita Mary Ramabai, Translator of the Scriptures, 1922*			
W		Acts 13. 13–25 Ps. 89. 1–2, 20–26 John 13. 16–20	Ps. 118 *alt.* Ps. 56; ***57***; (63†) Exod. 34. 1–10, 27–end Luke 4. 1–13	Ps. 81; ***85*** *alt.* Ps. 61; ***62***; 64 Deut. 11. 8–end Eph. 5. 15–end *or First EP of Philip and James:* Ps. 25 Isa. 40. 27–end John 12. 20–26 **R ct**

1 Friday	**PHILIP AND JAMES, APOSTLES**				
R			Isa. 30. 15–21 Ps. 119. 1–8 Eph. 1. 3–10 John 14. 1–14	*MP*: Ps. 139; 146 Prov. 4. 10–18 James 1. 1–12	*EP*: Ps. 149 Job 23. 1–12 John 1. 43–end
2 Saturday	**Athanasius, Bishop of Alexandria, Teacher, 373**				
W	Com. Teacher *also* Ecclus. 4. 20–28 Matt. 10. 24–27	*or*	Acts 13. 44–end Ps. 98. 1–5 John 14. 7–14	Ps. 34 *alt.* Ps. 68 Exod. 40. 17–end Luke 4. 31–37	Ps. ***84***; 86 *alt.* Ps. 65; ***66*** Deut. 15. 1–18 Eph. 6. 10–end **ct**
3 Sunday	**THE FIFTH SUNDAY OF EASTER**				
W	*The reading from Acts must be used as either the first or second reading at the Principal Service.*		Acts 7. 55–end [*or* Gen. 8. 1–19] Ps. 31. 1–5, 15–16 (*or* 31. 1–5) 1 Pet. 2. 2–10 John 14. 1–14	Ps. 30 Ezek. 37. 1–12 John 5. 19–29	Ps. 147. 1–12 Zech. 4. 1–10 Rev. 21. 1–14 *Gospel*: Luke 2. 25–32 [33–38]

May 2026		Sunday Principal Service Weekday Eucharist	Third Service Morning Prayer	Second Service Evening Prayer
4 Monday	**English Saints and Martyrs of the Reformation Era**			
W	Isa. 43. 1–7 *or* Ecclus. 2. 10–17 Ps. 87 2 Cor. 4. 5–12 John 12. 20–26	*or* Acts 14. 5–18 Ps. 118. 1–3, 14–15 John 14. 21–26	Ps. 145 *alt.* Ps. 71 Num. 9. 15–end; 10. 33–end Luke 4. 38–end	Ps. 105 *alt.* Ps. ***72***; 75 Deut. 16. 1–20 1 Pet. 1. 1–12
5 Tuesday				
W		Acts 14. 19–end Ps. 145. 10–end John 14. 27–end	Ps. ***19***; 147. 1–12 *alt.* Ps. 73 Num. 11. 1–33 Luke 5. 1–11	Ps. 96; ***97*** *alt.* Ps. 74 Deut. 17. 8–end 1 Pet. 1. 13–end
6 Wednesday				
W		Acts 15. 1–6 Ps. 122. 1–5 John 15. 1–8	Ps. ***30***; 147. 13–end *alt.* Ps. 77 Num. ch. 12 Luke 5. 12–26	Ps. 98; ***99***; 100 *alt.* Ps. 119. 81–104 Deut. 18. 9–end 1 Pet. 2. 1–10

7 Thursday					
W			Acts 15. 7–21 Ps. 96. 1–3, 7–10 John 15. 9–11	Ps. ***57***; 148 *alt.* Ps. 78. 1–39† Num. 13. 1–3, 17–end Luke 5. 27–end	Ps. 104 *alt.* Ps. 78. 40–end† Deut. ch. 19 1 Pet. 2. 11–end
8 Friday	**Julian of Norwich, Spiritual Writer, c. 1417**				
W	Com. Religious *also* 1 Cor. 13. 8–end Matt. 5. 13–16	*or*	Acts 15. 22–31 Ps. 57. 8–end John 15. 12–17	Ps. ***138***; 149 *alt.* Ps. 55 Num. 14. 1–25 Luke 6. 1–11	Ps. 66 *alt.* Ps. 69 Deut. 21.22 – 22.8 1 Pet. 3. 1–12
9 Saturday					
W			Acts 16. 1–10 Ps. 100 John 15. 18–21	Ps. ***146***; 150 *alt.* Ps. ***76***; 79 Num. 14. 26–end Luke 6. 12–26	Ps. 118 *alt.* Ps. 81; ***84*** Deut. 24. 5–end 1 Pet. 3. 13–end **ct**

		Sunday Principal Service Weekday Eucharist	Third Service Morning Prayer	Second Service Evening Prayer
10 Sunday	**THE SIXTH SUNDAY OF EASTER**			
W	*The reading from Acts must be used as either the first or second reading at the Principal Service.*	Acts 17. 22–31 [*or* Gen. 8.20 – 9.17] Ps. 66. 7–end 1 Pet. 3. 13–end John 14. 15–21	Ps. 73. 21–28 Job 14. 1–2, 7–15; 19. 23–27a 1 Thess. 4. 13–end	Ps. 87; 36. 5–10 Zech. 8. 1–13 Rev. 21.22 – 22.5 *Gospel*: John 21. 1–14
11 Monday	Rogation Day			
W		Acts 16. 11–15 Ps. 149. 1–5 John 15.26 – 16.4	Ps. ***65***; 67 *alt.* Ps. ***80***; 82 Num. 16. 1–35 Luke 6. 27–38	Ps. ***121***; 122; 123 *alt.* Ps. ***85***; 86 Deut. ch. 26 1 Pet. 4. 1–11
12 Tuesday	Rogation Day *Gregory Dix, Priest, Monk, Scholar, 1952*			
W		Acts 16. 22–34 Ps. 138 John 16. 5–11	Ps. 124; 125; ***126***; 127 *alt.* Ps. 87; ***89. 1–18*** Num. 16. 36–end Luke 6. 39–end	Ps. ***128***; 129; 130; 131 *alt.* Ps. 89. 19–end Deut. 28. 1–14 1 Pet. 4. 12–end

13 Wednesday Rogation Day

W		Acts 17.15, 22 – 18.1 Ps. 148. 1–2, 11–end John 16. 12–15	Ps. ***132***; 133 *alt.* Ps. 119. 105–128 Num. 17. 1–11 Luke 7. 1–10	*First EP of Ascension Day* Ps. 15; 24 2 Sam. 23. 1–5 Col. 2.20 – 3.4 **𝔚 ct**

14 Thursday **ASCENSION DAY** (Matthias transferred to 15 May)

𝔚	*The reading from Acts must be used as either the first or second reading at the Eucharist.*	Acts 1. 1–11 *or* Dan. 7. 9–14 Ps. 47 *or* Ps. 93 Eph. 1. 15–end *or* Acts 1. 1–11 Luke 24. 44–end	*MP*: Ps. 110; 150 Isa. 52. 7–end Heb. 7. [11–25] 26–end	*EP*: Ps. 8 Song of the Three 29–37 *or* 2 Kings 2. 1–15 Rev. ch. 5 *Gospel*: Mark 16. 14–end

		Sunday Principal Service Weekday Eucharist	Third Service Morning Prayer	Second Service Evening Prayer
15 Friday	**MATTHIAS THE APOSTLE***			
R		Isa. 22. 15–end *or* Acts 1. 15–end Ps. 15 Acts 1. 15–end *or* 1 Cor. 4. 1–7 John 15. 9–17	*MP*: Ps. 16; 147. 1–12 1 Sam. 2. 27–35 Acts 2. 37–end	*EP*: Ps. 80 1 Sam. 16. 1–13a Matt. 7. 15–27
	or, if Matthias is celebrated on 24 February:			
W		Acts 18. 9–18 Ps. 47. 1–6 John 16. 20–23	Ps. 20; ***81*** *alt*. Ps. ***88***; (95) Num. 20. 1–13 Luke 7. 11–17 [Exod. 35.30 – 36.1 Gal. 5. 13–end]**	Ps. 145 *alt*. Ps. 102 Deut. 29. 2–15 1 John 1.1 – 2.6
16 Saturday	*Caroline Chisholm, Social Reformer, 1877*			
W		Acts 18. 22–end Ps. 47. 1–2, 7–end John 16. 23–28	Ps. 21; ***47*** *alt*. Ps. 96; ***97***; 100 Num. 21. 4–9 Luke 7. 18–35 [Num. 11. 16–17, 24–29 1 Cor. ch. 2]**	Ps. 84; ***85*** *alt*. Ps. 104 Deut. ch. 30 1 John 2. 7–17 **ct**

17 Sunday	**THE SEVENTH SUNDAY OF EASTER (SUNDAY AFTER ASCENSION DAY)**			
W	*The reading from Acts must be used as either the first or second reading at the Principal Service.*	Acts 1. 6–14 [*or* Ezek. 36. 24–28] Ps. 68. 1–10, 32–end (*or* 68. 1–10) 1 Pet. 4. 12–14; 5. 6–11 John 17. 1–11	Ps. 104. 26–35 Isa. 65. 17–end Rev. 21. 1–8	Ps. 47 2 Sam. 23. 1–5 Eph. 1. 15–end *Gospel*: Mark 16. 14–end
18 Monday				
W		Acts 19. 1–8 Ps. 68. 1–6 John 16. 29–end	Ps. ***93***; 96; 97 *alt*. Ps. ***98***; 99; 101 Num. 22. 1–35 Luke 7. 36–end [Num. 27. 15–end 1 Cor. ch. 3]***	Ps. 18 *alt*. Ps. ***105***† (*or* 103) Deut. 31. 1–13 1 John 2. 18–end

*Matthias may be celebrated on 24 February instead of 15 May.
**The alternative readings in square brackets may be used at one of the offices, in preparation for the Day of Pentecost.

			Sunday Principal Service Weekday Eucharist	Third Service Morning Prayer	Second Service Evening Prayer
19 Tuesday	**Dunstan, Archbishop of Canterbury, Restorer of Monastic Life, 988**				
W	Com. Bishop *esp.* Matt. 24. 42–46 *also* Exod. 31. 1–5	*or*	Acts 20. 17–27 Ps. 68. 9–10, 18–19 John 17. 1–11	Ps. 98; ***99***; 100 *alt.* Ps. ***106***† (*or* 103) Num. 22.36 – 23.12 Luke 8. 1–15 [1 Sam. 10. 1–10 1 Cor. 12. 1–13]*	Ps. 68 *alt.* Ps. 107† Deut. 31. 14–29 1 John 3. 1–10
20 Wednesday	**Alcuin of York, Deacon, Abbot of Tours, 804**				
W	Com. Religious *also* Col. 3. 12–16 John 4. 19–24	*or*	Acts 20. 28–end Ps. 68. 27–28, 32–end John 17. 11–19	Ps. 2; ***29*** *alt.* Ps. 110; ***111***; 112 Num. 23. 13–end Luke 8. 16–25 [1 Kings 19. 1–18 Matt. 3. 13–end]*	Ps. 36; ***46*** *alt.* Ps. 119. 129–152 Deut. 31.30 – 32.14 1 John 3. 11–end

21 Thursday *Helena, Protector of the Holy Places, 330*			
W	Acts 22. 30; 23. 6–11 Ps. 16. 1, 5–end John 17. 20–end	Ps. ***24***; 72 *alt*. Ps. 113; ***115*** Num. ch. 24 Luke 8. 26–39 [Ezek. 11. 14–20 Matt. 9.35 – 10.20]*	Ps. 139 *alt*. Ps. 114; ***116***; 117 Deut. 32. 15–47 1 John 4. 1–6
22 Friday			
W	Acts 25. 13–21 Ps. 103. 1–2, 11–12, 19–20 John 21. 15–19	Ps. ***28***; 30 *alt*. Ps. 139 Num. 27. 12–end Luke 8. 40–end [Ezek. 36. 22–28 Matt. 12. 22–32]*	Ps. 147 *alt*. Ps. ***130***; 131; 137 Deut. ch. 33 1 John 4. 7–end
23 Saturday			
W	Acts 28. 16–20, 30–end Ps. 11. 4–end John 21. 20–end	Ps. 42; ***43*** *alt*. Ps. 120; ***121***; 122 Num. 32. 1–27 Luke 9. 1–17 [Mic. 3. 1–8 Eph. 6. 10–20]*	*First EP of Pentecost* Ps. 48 Deut. 16. 9–15 John 15.26 – 16.15 **R ct**

*The alternative readings in square brackets may be used at one of the offices, in preparation for the Day of Pentecost.

		Sunday Principal Service Weekday Eucharist	Third Service Morning Prayer	Second Service Evening Prayer
24 Sunday	**DAY OF PENTECOST (Whit Sunday)**			
R	*The reading from Acts must be used as either the first or second reading at the Principal Service.*	Acts 2. 1–21 *or* Num. 11. 24–30 Ps. 104. 26–36, 37b (*or* 104. 26–end) 1 Cor. 12. 3b–13 *or* Acts 2. 1–21 John 20. 19–23 *or* John 7. 37–39	*MP*: Ps. 87 Gen. 11. 1–9 Acts 10. 34–end	*EP*: Ps. 67; 133 Joel 2. 21–end Acts 2. 14–21 [22–38] *Gospel*: Luke 24. 44–end
25 Monday	**The Venerable Bede, Monk at Jarrow, Scholar, Historian, 735** *Aldhelm, Bishop of Sherborne, 709* Ordinary Time resumes today			
Gw **DEL 8**	Com. Religious *or* *also* Ecclus. 39. 1–10	1 Pet. 1. 3–9 Ps. 111 Mark 10. 17–27	Ps. 123; 124; 125; ***126*** Josh. ch. 1 Luke 9. 18–27	Ps. ***127***; 128; 129 2 Chron. 17. 1–12 Rom. 1. 1–17
26 Tuesday	**Augustine, first Archbishop of Canterbury, 605** *John Calvin, Reformer, 1564; Philip Neri, Founder of the Oratorians, Spiritual Guide, 1595*			
Gw	Com. Bishop *or* *also* 1 Thess. 2. 2b–8 Matt. 13. 31–33	1 Pet. 1. 10–16 Ps. 98. 1–5 Mark 10. 28–31	Ps. ***132***; 133 Josh. ch. 2 Luke 9. 28–36	Ps. (134); ***135*** 2 Chron. 18. 1–27 Rom. 1. 18–end

27 Wednesday

G			1 Pet. 1. 18–end Ps. 147. 13–end Mark 10. 32–45	Ps. 119. 153–end Josh. ch. 3 Luke 9. 37–50	Ps. 136 2 Chron. 18.28 – 19.end Rom. 2. 1–16

28 Thursday *Lanfranc, Prior of Le Bec, Archbishop of Canterbury, Scholar, 1089*

G			1 Pet. 2. 2–5, 9–12 Ps. 100 Mark 10. 46–end	Ps. ***143***; 146 Josh. 4.1 – 5.1 Luke 9. 51–end	Ps. ***138***; 140; 141 2 Chron. 20. 1–23 Rom. 2. 17–end

29 Friday

G			1 Pet. 4. 7–13 Ps. 96. 10–end Mark 11. 11–26	Ps. ***142***; 144 Josh. 5. 2–end Luke 10. 1–16	Ps. 145 2 Chron. 22.10 – 23.end Rom. 3. 1–20

30 Saturday **Josephine Butler, Social Reformer, 1906**
Joan of Arc, Visionary, 1431; Apolo Kivebulaya, Priest, Evangelist in Central Africa, 1933

Gw	Com. Saint *esp.* Isa. 58. 6–11 *also* 1 John 3. 18–23 Matt. 9. 10–13	*or*	Jude 17, 20–end Ps. 63. 1–6 Mark 11. 27–end	Ps. 147 Josh. 6. 1–20 Luke 10. 17–24	*First EP of Trinity Sunday* Ps. 97; 98 Exod. 34. 1–10 Mark 1. 1–13 **𝔚 ct**

		Sunday Principal Service Weekday Eucharist	Third Service Morning Prayer	Second Service Evening Prayer
31 Sunday	**TRINITY SUNDAY** (Visitation transferred to 1 June)			
𝔚		Isa. 40. 12–17, 27–end Ps. 8 2 Cor. 13. 11–end Matt. 28. 16–end	*MP*: Ps. 86. 8–13 Exod. 3. 1–6, 13–15 John 17. 1–11	*EP*: Ps. 93; 150 Isa. 6. 1–8 John 16. 5–15

June 2026

		Sunday Principal Service Weekday Eucharist	Third Service Morning Prayer	Second Service Evening Prayer
1 Monday	**THE VISIT OF THE BLESSED VIRGIN MARY TO ELIZABETH** (transferred from 31 May)*			
W **DEL 9**		Zeph. 3. 14–18 Ps. 113 Rom. 12. 9–16 Luke 1. 39–49 [50–56]	*MP*: Ps. 85; 150 1 Sam. 2. 1–10 Mark 3. 31–end	*EP*: Ps. 122; 127; 128 Zech. 2. 10–end John 3. 25–30
	or, if The Visitation is celebrated on 2 July: **Justin, Martyr at Rome, c. 165**			
Gr	Com. Martyr *esp.* John 15. 18–21 *also* 1 Macc. 2. 15–22 1 Cor. 1. 18–25	*or* 2 Pet. 1. 2–7 Ps. 91. 1–2, 14–end Mark 12. 1–12	Ps. ***1***; 2; 3 Josh. 7. 1–15 Luke 10. 25–37	Ps. ***4***; 7 2 Chron. 26. 1–21 Rom. 4. 1–12

2 Tuesday

G	2 Pet. 3. 11–15a, 17–end Ps. 90. 1–4, 10, 14, 16 Mark 12. 13–17	Ps. ***5***; 6; (8) Josh. 7. 16–end Luke 10. 38–end	Ps. ***9***; 10† 2 Chron. ch. 28 Rom. 4. 13–end

3 Wednesday *The Martyrs of Uganda, 1885–87 and 1977*

G	2 Tim. 1. 1–3, 6–12 Ps. 123 Mark 12. 18–27	Ps. 119. 1–32 Josh. 8. 1–29 Luke 11. 1–13	Ps. ***11***; 12; 13 2 Chron. 29. 1–19 Rom. 5. 1–11 *or First EP of Corpus Christi* Ps. 110; 111 Exod. 16. 2–15 John 6. 22–35 **W ct**

*The Visit of the Blessed Virgin Mary to Elizabeth may be celebrated on 2 July instead of 1 June.

		Sunday Principal Service Weekday Eucharist	Third Service Morning Prayer	Second Service Evening Prayer
4 Thursday	**DAY OF THANKSGIVING FOR HOLY COMMUNION (CORPUS CHRISTI)** *Petroc, Abbot of Padstow, 6th century*			
W		Gen. 14. 18–20 Ps. 116. 10–end 1 Cor. 11. 23–26 John 6. 51–58	*MP*: Ps. 147 Deut. 8. 2–16 1 Cor. 10. 1–17	*EP*: Ps. 23; 42; 43 Prov. 9. 1–5 Luke 9. 11–17
	or, if Corpus Christi is not observed:			
G		2 Tim. 2. 8–15 Ps. 25. 4–12 Mark 12. 28–34	Ps. 14; ***15***; 16 Josh. 8. 30–end Luke 11. 14–28	Ps. 18† 2 Chron. 29. 20–end Rom. 5. 12–end
5 Friday	**Boniface (Wynfrith) of Crediton, Bishop, Apostle of Germany, Martyr, 754**			
Gr	Com. Martyr *also* Acts 20. 24–28 *or*	2 Tim. 3. 10–end Ps. 119. 161–168 Mark 12. 35–37	Ps. 17; ***19*** Josh. 9. 3–26 Luke 11. 29–36	Ps. 22 2 Chron. ch. 30 Rom. 6. 1–14
6 Saturday	*Ini Kopuria, Founder of the Melanesian Brotherhood, 1945*			
G		2 Tim. 4. 1–8 Ps. 71. 7–16 Mark 12. 38–end	Ps. 20; 21; ***23*** Josh. 10. 1–15 Luke 11. 37–end	Ps. ***24***; 25 2 Chron. 32. 1–22 Rom. 6. 15–end **ct**

7 Sunday	**THE FIRST SUNDAY AFTER TRINITY (Proper 5)**				
G	*Track 1* Gen. 12. 1–9 Ps. 33. 1–12 Rom. 4. 13–end Matt. 9. 9–13, 18–26		*Track 2* Hos. 5.15 – 6.6 Ps. 50. 7–15 Rom. 4. 13–25 Matt. 9. 9–13, 18–26	Ps. 38 Deut. 6. 10–25 Acts 22.22 – 23.11	Ps. [39]; 41 1 Sam. 18. 1–16 Luke 8. 41–56
8 Monday	**Thomas Ken, Bishop of Bath and Wells, Nonjuror, Hymn Writer, 1711**				
Gw **DEL 10**	Com. Bishop *esp.* 2 Cor. 4. 1–10 Matt. 24. 42–46	*or*	1 Kings 17. 1–6 Ps. 121 Matt. 5. 1–12	Ps. 27; ***30*** Josh. ch. 14 Luke 12. 1–12	Ps. 26; ***28***; 29 2 Chron. 33. 1–13 Rom. 7. 1–6
9 Tuesday	**Columba, Abbot of Iona, Missionary, 597** *Ephrem of Syria, Deacon, Hymn Writer, Teacher, 373*				
Gw	Com. Missionary *also* Titus 2. 11–end	*or*	1 Kings 17. 7–16 Ps. 4 Matt. 5. 13–16	Ps. 32; ***36*** Josh. 21.43 – 22.8 Luke 12. 13–21	Ps. 33 2 Chron. 34. 1–18 Rom. 7. 7–end

		Sunday Principal Service Weekday Eucharist	Third Service Morning Prayer	Second Service Evening Prayer
10 Wednesday				
G		1 Kings 18. 20–39 Ps. 16. 1, 6–end Matt. 5. 17–19	Ps. 34 Josh. 22. 9–end Luke 12. 22–31	Ps. 119. 33–56 2 Chron. 34. 19–end Rom. 8. 1–11 *or First EP of Barnabas* Ps. 1; 15 Isa. 42. 5–12 Acts 14. 8–end **R ct**
11 Thursday	**BARNABAS THE APOSTLE**			
R		Job 29. 11–16 *or* Acts 11. 19–end Ps. 112 Acts 11. 19–end *or* Gal. 2. 1–10 John 15. 12–17	*MP*: Ps. 100; 101; 117 Jer. 9. 23–24 Acts 4. 32–end	*EP*: Ps. 147 Eccles. 12. 9–end *or* Tobit 4. 5–11 Acts 9. 26–31
12 Friday				
G		1 Kings 19. 9, 11–16 Ps. 27. 8–16 Matt. 5. 27–32	Ps. 31 Josh. 24. 1–28 Luke 12. 41–48	Ps. 35 2 Chron. 35.20 – 36.10 Rom. 8. 18–30

13 Saturday				
G		1 Kings 19. 19–end Ps. 16. 1–7 Matt. 5. 33–37	Ps. 41; ***42***; 43 Josh. 24. 29–end Luke 12. 49–end	Ps. 45; ***46*** 2 Chron. 36. 11–end Rom. 8. 31–end **ct**
14 Sunday	**THE SECOND SUNDAY AFTER TRINITY (Proper 6)**			
G	*Track 1* Gen. 18. 1–15 [21. 1–7] Ps. 116. 1, 10–17 (*or* 116. 9–17) Rom. 5. 1–8 Matt. 9.35 – 10.8 [9–23]	*Track 2* Exod. 19. 2–8a Ps. 100 Rom. 5. 1–8 Matt. 9.35 – 10.8 [9–23]	Ps. 45 Deut. 10.12 – 11.1 Acts 23. 12–end	Ps. [42]; 43 1 Sam. 21. 1–15 Luke 11. 14–28
15 Monday	*Evelyn Underhill, Spiritual Writer, 1941*			
G **DEL 11**		1 Kings 21. 1–16 Ps. 5. 1–5 Matt. 5. 38–42	Ps. 44 Judg. ch. 2 Luke 13. 1–9	Ps. ***47***; 49 Ezra ch. 1 Rom. 9. 1–18

June 2026		Sunday Principal Service Weekday Eucharist	Third Service Morning Prayer	Second Service Evening Prayer
16 Tuesday	**Richard, Bishop of Chichester, 1253** *Joseph Butler, Bishop of Durham, Philosopher, 1752*			
Gw	Com. Bishop *or* *also* John 21. 15–19	1 Kings 21. 17–end Ps. 51. 1–9 Matt. 5. 43–end	Ps. ***48***; 52 Judg. 4. 1–23 Luke 13. 10–21	Ps. 50 Ezra ch. 3 Rom. 9. 19–end
17 Wednesday	*Samuel and Henrietta Barnett, Social Reformers, 1913 and 1936*			
G		2 Kings 2. 1, 6–14 Ps. 31. 21–end Matt. 6. 1–6, 16–18	Ps. 119. 57–80 Judg. ch. 5 Luke 13. 22–end	Ps. ***59***; 60; (67) Ezra 4. 1–5 Rom. 10. 1–10
18 Thursday	*Bernard Mizeki, Apostle of the MaShona, Martyr, 1896*			
G		Ecclus. 48. 1–14 *or* Isa. 63. 7–9 Ps. 97. 1–8 Matt. 6. 7–15	Ps. 56; ***57***; (63†) Judg. 6. 1–24 Luke 14. 1–11	Ps. 61; ***62***; 64 Ezra 4. 7–end Rom. 10. 11–end
19 Friday	*Sundar Singh of India, Sadhu (holy man), Evangelist, Teacher, 1929*			
G		2 Kings 11. 1–4, 9–18, 20 Ps. 132. 1–5, 11–13 Matt. 6. 19–23	Ps. ***51***; 54 Judg. 6. 25–end Luke 14. 12–24	Ps. 38 Ezra ch. 5 Rom. 11. 1–12

20 Saturday				
G		2 Chron. 24. 17–25 Ps. 89. 25–33 Matt. 6. 24–end	Ps. 68 Judg. ch. 7 Luke 14. 25–end	Ps. 65; ***66*** Ezra ch. 6 Rom. 11. 13–24 **ct**
21 Sunday	**THE THIRD SUNDAY AFTER TRINITY (Proper 7)**			
G	*Track 1* Gen. 21. 8–21 Ps. 86. 1–10, 16–end (*or* 86. 1–10) Rom. 6. 1b–11 Matt. 10. 24–39	*Track 2* Jer. 20. 7–13 Ps. 69. 8–11 [12–17] 18–20 (*or* 69. 14–20) Rom. 6. 1b–11 Matt. 10. 24–39	Ps. 49 Deut. 11. 1–15 Acts 27. 1–12	Ps. 46; [48] 1 Sam. 24. 1–17 Luke 14. 12–24
22 Monday	**Alban, first Martyr of Britain, c. 250**			
Gr **DEL 12**	Com. Martyr *esp.* 2 Tim. 2. 3–13 John 12. 24–26	*or* 2 Kings 17. 5–8, 13–15, 18 Ps. 60. 1–5, 11–end Matt. 7. 1–5	Ps. 71 Judg. 8. 22–end Luke 15. 1–10	Ps. ***72***; 75 Ezra ch. 7 Rom. 11. 25–end

June 2026		Sunday Principal Service Weekday Eucharist	Third Service Morning Prayer	Second Service Evening Prayer
23 Tuesday	**Etheldreda, Abbess of Ely, c. 678**			
Gw	Com. Religious *also* Matt. 25. 1–13 *or*	2 Kings 19. 9b–11, 14–21, 31–36 Ps. 48. 1–2, 8–end Matt. 7. 6, 12–14	Ps. 73 Judg. 9. 1–21 Luke 15. 11–end	Ps. 74 Ezra 8. 15–end Rom. 12. 1–8 *or First EP of The Birth of John the Baptist* Ps. 71 Judg. 13. 2–7, 24–end Luke 1. 5–25 **W ct**
24 Wednesday	**THE BIRTH OF JOHN THE BAPTIST** Ember Day			
W		Isa. 40. 1–11 Ps. 85. 7–end Acts 13. 14b–26 *or* Gal. 3. 23–end Luke 1. 57–66, 80	*MP*: Ps. 50; 149 Ecclus. 48. 1–10 *or* Mal. 3. 1–6 Luke 3. 1–17	*EP*: Ps. 80; 82 Mal. ch. 4 Matt. 11. 2–19

25 Thursday				
G		2 Kings 24. 8–17 Ps. 79. 1–9, 12 Matt. 7. 21–end	Ps. 78. 1–39† Judg. 11. 1–11 Luke 16. 19–end	Ps. 78. 40–end† Ezra 10. 1–17 Rom. 13. 1–7
26 Friday	Ember Day			
G *or* **R**		2 Kings 25. 1–12 Ps. 137. 1–6 Matt. 8. 1–4	Ps. 55 Judg. 11. 29–end Luke 17. 1–10	Ps. 69 Neh. ch. 1 Rom. 13. 8–end
27 Saturday	Ember Day *Cyril, Bishop of Alexandria, Teacher, 444*			
G *or* **R**		Lam. 2. 2, 10–14, 18–19 Ps. 74. 1–3, 21–end Matt. 8. 5–17	Ps. ***76***; 79 Judg. 12. 1–7 Luke 17. 11–19	Ps. 81; ***84*** Neh. ch. 2 Rom. 14. 1–12 **ct**

		Sunday Principal Service Weekday Eucharist	Third Service Morning Prayer	Second Service Evening Prayer
28 Sunday	**THE FOURTH SUNDAY AFTER TRINITY (Proper 8)**			
G	*Track 1* Gen. 22. 1–14 Ps. 13 Rom. 6. 12–end Matt. 10. 40–end	*Track 2* Jer. 28. 5–9 Ps. 89. 1–4, 15–18 (*or* 89. 8–18) Rom. 6. 12–end Matt. 10. 40–end	Ps. 52; 53 Deut. 15. 1–11 Acts 27. [13–32] 33–end	Ps. 50 (*or* 50. 1–15) 1 Sam. 28. 3–19 Luke 17. 20–end *or First EP of Peter and Paul* Ps. 66; 67 Ezek. 3. 4–11 Gal. 1.13 – 2.8 *or, for Peter alone*: Acts 9. 32–end **R ct**
29 Monday	**PETER AND PAUL, APOSTLES**			
R **DEL 13**		Zech. 4. 1–6a, 10b–end *or* Acts 12. 1–11 Ps. 125 Acts 12. 1–11 *or* 2 Tim. 4. 6–8, 17–18 Matt. 16. 13–19	*MP*: Ps. 71; 113 Isa. 49. 1–6 Acts 11. 1–18	*EP*: Ps. 124; 138 Ezek. 34. 11–16 John 21. 15–22

or, if Peter is commemorated alone:

	Ezek. 3. 22–end *or* Acts 12. 1–11 Ps. 125 Acts 12. 1–11 *or* 1 Pet. 2. 19–end Matt. 16. 13–19	*MP*: Ps. 71; 113 Isa. 49. 1–6 Acts 11. 1–18	*EP*: Ps. 124; 138 Ezek. 34. 11–16 John 21. 15–22

30 Tuesday

G	Amos 3. 1–8; 4. 11–12 Ps. 5. 8–end Matt. 8. 23–27	Ps. 87; ***89. 1–18*** Judg. ch. 14 Luke 18. 1–14	Ps. 89. 19–end Neh. ch. 5 Rom. 15. 1–13

July 2026

1 Wednesday *Henry, John and Henry Venn the Younger, Priests, Evangelical Divines, 1797, 1813 and 1873*

G	Amos 5. 14–15, 21–24 Ps. 50. 7–14 Matt. 8. 28–end	Ps. 119. 105–128 Judg. 15.1 – 16.3 Luke 18. 15–30	Ps. ***91***; 93 Neh. 6.1 – 7.4 Rom. 15. 14–21

July 2026		Sunday Principal Service Weekday Eucharist	Third Service Morning Prayer	Second Service Evening Prayer
2 Thursday*				
G		Amos 7. 10–end Ps. 19. 7–10 Matt. 9. 1–8	Ps. 90; **92** Judg. 16. 4–end Luke 18. 31–end	Ps. 94 Neh. 7.73b – 8.end Rom. 15. 22–end *or First EP of Thomas* Ps. 27 Isa. ch. 35 Heb. 10.35 – 11.1 **R ct**
3 Friday	**THOMAS THE APOSTLE****			
R		Hab. 2. 1–4 Ps. 31. 1–6 Eph. 2. 19–end John 20. 24–29	*MP*: Ps. 92; 146 2 Sam. 15. 17–21 *or* Ecclus. ch. 2 John 11. 1–16	*EP*: Ps. 139 Job 42. 1–6 1 Pet. 1. 3–12
	or, if Thomas is not celebrated:			
G		Amos 8. 4–6, 9–12 Ps. 119. 1–8 Matt. 9. 9–13	Ps. ***88***; (95) Judg. ch. 17 Luke 19. 1–10	Ps. 102 Neh. 9. 1–23 Rom. 16. 1–16

4 Saturday				
G		Amos 9. 11–end Ps. 85. 8–end Matt. 9. 14–17	Ps. 96; **97**; 100 Judg. 18. 1–20, 27–end Luke 19. 11–27	Ps. 104 Neh. 9. 24–end Rom. 16. 17–end **ct**
5 Sunday	**THE FIFTH SUNDAY AFTER TRINITY (Proper 9)**			
G	*Track 1* Gen. 24. 34–38, 42–49, 58–end Ps. 45. 10–end *or Canticle*: Song of Sol. 2. 8–13 Rom. 7. 15–25a Matt. 11. 16–19, 25–end	*Track 2* Zech. 9. 9–12 Ps. 145. 8–15 Rom. 7. 15–25a Matt. 11. 16–19, 25–end	Ps. 55. 1–15, 18–22 Deut. 24. 10–end Acts 28. 1–16	Ps. 56; [57] 2 Sam. 2. 1–11; 3. 1 Luke 18.31 – 19.10
6 Monday	*Thomas More, Scholar, and John Fisher, Bishop of Rochester, Reformation Martyrs, 1535*			
G **DEL 14**		Hos. 2. 14–16, 19–20 Ps. 145. 2–9 Matt. 9. 18–26	Ps. **98**; 99; 101 1 Sam. 1. 1–20 Luke 19. 28–40	Ps. ***105***† (*or* 103) Neh. 12. 27–47 2 Cor. 1. 1–14

*The Visit of the Blessed Virgin Mary to Elizabeth may be celebrated on 2 July instead of 1 June.
**Thomas the Apostle may be celebrated on 21 December instead of 3 July.

July 2026		Sunday Principal Service Weekday Eucharist	Third Service Morning Prayer	Second Service Evening Prayer
7 Tuesday*				
	G	Hos. 8. 4–7, 11–13 Ps. 103. 8–12 Matt. 9. 32–end	Ps. ***106***† (*or* 103) 1 Sam. 1.21 – 2.11 Luke 19. 41–end	Ps. 107† Neh. 13. 1–14 2 Cor. 1.15 – 2.4
8 Wednesday				
	G	Hos. 10. 1–3, 7–8, 12 Ps. 115. 3–10 Matt. 10. 1–7	Ps. 110; ***111***; 112 1 Sam. 2. 12–26 Luke 20. 1–8	Ps. 119. 129–152 Neh. 13. 15–end 2 Cor. 2. 5–end
9 Thursday				
	G	Hos. 11. 1, 3–4, 8–9 Ps. 105. 1–7 Matt. 10. 7–15	Ps. 113; ***115*** 1 Sam. 2. 27–end Luke 20. 9–19	Ps. 114; ***116***; 117 Esther ch. 1 2 Cor. ch. 3
10 Friday				
	G	Hos. 14. 2–end Ps. 80. 1–7 Matt. 10. 16–23	Ps. 139 1 Sam. 3.1 – 4.1a Luke 20. 20–26	Ps. ***130***; 131; 137 Esther ch. 2 2 Cor. ch. 4

11 Saturday	**Benedict of Nursia, Abbot of Monte Cassino, Father of Western Monasticism, c. 550**			
Gw	Com. Religious *also* 1 Cor. 3. 10–11 Luke 18. 18–22	*or* Isa. 6. 1–8 Ps. 51. 1–7 Matt. 10. 24–33	Ps. 120; ***121***; 122 1 Sam. 4. 1b–end Luke 20. 27–40	Ps. 118 Esther ch. 3 2 Cor. ch. 5 **ct**
12 Sunday	**THE SIXTH SUNDAY AFTER TRINITY (Proper 10)**			
G	*Track 1* Gen. 25. 19–end Ps. 119. 105–112 Rom. 8. 1–11 Matt. 13. 1–9, 18–23	*Track 2* Isa. 55. 10–13 Ps. 65 (*or* 65. 8–end) Rom. 8. 1–11 Matt. 13. 1–9, 18–23	Ps. 64; 65 Deut. 28. 1–14 Acts 28. 17–end	Ps. 60; [63] 2 Sam. 7. 18–end Luke 19.41 – 20.8
13 Monday				
G **DEL 15**		Isa. 1. 11–17 Ps. 50. 7–15 Matt. 10.34 – 11.1	Ps. 123; 124; 125; ***126*** 1 Sam. ch. 5 Luke 20.41 – 21.4	Ps. ***127***; 128; 129 Esther ch. 4 2 Cor. 6.1 – 7.1

*Thomas Becket may be celebrated on 7 July instead of 29 December.

July 2026		Sunday Principal Service Weekday Eucharist	Third Service Morning Prayer	Second Service Evening Prayer
14 Tuesday	**John Keble, Priest, Tractarian, Poet, 1866**			
Gw	Com. Pastor *or* *also* Lam. 3. 19–26 Matt. 5. 1–8	Isa. 7. 1–9 Ps. 48. 1–7 Matt. 11. 20–24	Ps. ***132***; 133 1 Sam. 6. 1–16 Luke 21. 5–19	Ps. (134); ***135*** Esther ch. 5 2 Cor. 7. 2–end
15 Wednesday	**Swithun, Bishop of Winchester, c. 862** *Bonaventure, Friar, Bishop, Teacher, 1274*			
Gw	Com. Bishop *or* *also* James 5. 7–11, 13–18	Isa. 10. 5–7, 13–16 Ps. 94. 5–11 Matt. 11. 25–27	Ps. 119. 153–end 1 Sam. ch. 7 Luke 21. 20–28	Ps. 136 Esther 6. 1–13 2 Cor. 8. 1–15
16 Thursday	*Osmund, Bishop of Salisbury, 1099*			
G		Isa. 26. 7–9, 16–19 Ps. 102. 14–21 Matt. 11. 28–end	Ps. ***143***; 146 1 Sam. ch. 8 Luke 21. 29–end	Ps. ***138***; 140; 141 Esther 6.14 – 7.end 2 Cor. 8.16 – 9.5
17 Friday				
G		Isa. 38. 1–6, 21–22, 7–8 *Canticle*: Isa. 38. 10–16 *or* Ps. 32. 1–8 Matt. 12. 1–8	Ps. 142; ***144*** 1 Sam. 9. 1–14 Luke 22. 1–13	Ps. 145 Esther ch. 8 2 Cor. 9. 6–end

18 Saturday	*Elizabeth Ferard, first deaconess of the Church of England, Founder of the Community of St Andrew, 1883*			
G		Mic. 2. 1–5 Ps. 10. 1–5a, 12 Matt. 12. 14–21	Ps. 147 1 Sam. 9.15 – 10.1 Luke 22. 14–23	Ps. ***148***; 149; 150 Esther 9. 20–28 2 Cor. ch. 10 **ct**
19 Sunday	**THE SEVENTH SUNDAY AFTER TRINITY (Proper 11)**			
G	*Track 1* Gen. 28. 10–19a Ps. 139. 1–11, 23–24 (*or* 139. 1–11) Rom. 8. 12–25 Matt. 13. 24–30, 36–43	*Track 2* Wisd. 12. 13, 16–19 *or* Isa. 44. 6–8 Ps. 86. 11–end Rom. 8. 12–25 Matt. 13. 24–30, 36–43	Ps. 71 Deut. 30. 1–10 1 Pet. 3. 8–18	Ps. 67; [70] 1 Kings 2. 10–12; 3. 16–end Acts 4. 1–22 *Gospel*: Mark 6. 30–34, 53–end
20 Monday	*Margaret of Antioch, Martyr, 4th century; Bartolomé de las Casas, Apostle to the Indies, 1566*			
G **DEL 16**		Mic. 6. 1–4, 6–8 Ps. 50. 3–7, 14 Matt. 12. 38–42	Ps. ***1***; 2; 3 1 Sam. 10. 1–16 Luke 22. 24–30	Ps. ***4***; 7 Jer. ch. 26 2 Cor. 11. 1–15

July 2026		Sunday Principal Service Weekday Eucharist	Third Service Morning Prayer	Second Service Evening Prayer
21 Tuesday				
G		Mic. 7. 14–15, 18–20 Ps. 85. 1–7 Matt. 12. 46–end	Ps. ***5***; 6; (8) 1 Sam. 10. 17–end Luke 22. 31–38	Ps. **9**; 10† Jer. ch. 28 2 Cor. 11. 16–end *or First EP of Mary Magdalene* Ps. 139 Isa. 25. 1–9 2 Cor. 1. 3–7 **W ct**
22 Wednesday	**MARY MAGDALENE**			
W		Song of Sol. 3. 1–4 Ps. 42. 1–10 2 Cor. 5. 14–17 John 20. 1–2, 11–18	*MP*: Ps. 30; 32; 150 1 Sam. 16. 14–end Luke 8. 1–3	*EP*: Ps. 63 Zeph. 3. 14–end Mark 15.40 – 16.7
23 Thursday	*Bridget of Sweden, Abbess of Vadstena, 1373*			
G		Jer. 2. 1–3, 7–8, 12–13 Ps. 36. 5–10 Matt. 13. 10–17	Ps. 14; ***15***; 16 1 Sam. ch. 12 Luke 22. 47–62	Ps. 18† Jer. 30. 1–11 2 Cor. ch. 13

24 Friday

G	Jer. 3. 14–17 Ps. 23 *or Canticle*: Jer. 31. 10–13 Matt. 13. 18–23	Ps. 17; ***19*** 1 Sam. 13. 5–18 Luke 22. 63–end	Ps. 22 Jer. 30. 12–22 James 1. 1–11 *or First EP of James* Ps. 144 Deut. 30. 11–end Mark 5. 21–end **R ct**

25 Saturday **JAMES THE APOSTLE**

R	Jer. 45. 1–5 *or* Acts 11.27 – 12.2 Ps. 126 Acts 11.27 – 12.2 *or* 2 Cor. 4. 7–15 Matt. 20. 20–28	*MP*: Ps. 7; 29; 117 2 Kings 1. 9–15 Luke 9. 46–56	*EP*: Ps. 94 Jer. 26. 1–15 Mark 1. 14–20

July 2026		Sunday Principal Service Weekday Eucharist	Third Service Morning Prayer	Second Service Evening Prayer
26 Sunday	**THE EIGHTH SUNDAY AFTER TRINITY (Proper 12)**			
G	*Track 1* Gen. 29. 15–28 Ps. 105. 1–11, 45b (*or* 105. 1–11) *or* Ps. 128 Rom. 8. 26–end Matt. 13. 31–33, 44–52	*Track 2* 1 Kings 3. 5–12 Ps. 119. 129–136 Rom. 8. 26–end Matt. 13. 31–33, 44–52	Ps. 77 Song of Sol. ch. 2 *or* 1 Macc. 2. [1–14] 15–22 1 Pet. 4. 7–14	Ps. 75; [76] 1 Kings 6. 11–14, 23–end Acts 12. 1–17 *Gospel*: John 6. 1–21
27 Monday	*Brooke Foss Westcott, Bishop of Durham, Teacher, 1901*			
G **DEL 17**		Jer. 13. 1–11 Ps. 82 *or* Deut. 32. 18–21 Matt. 13. 31–35	Ps. 27; ***30*** 1 Sam. 14. 24–46 Luke 23. 13–25	Ps. 26; **28**; 29 Jer. 31. 23–25, 27–37 James 2. 1–13
28 Tuesday				
G		Jer. 14. 17–end Ps. 79. 8–end Matt. 13. 36–43	Ps. 32; ***36*** 1 Sam. 15. 1–23 Luke 23. 26–43	Ps. 33 Jer. 32. 1–15 James 2. 14–end

29 Wednesday **Mary, Martha and Lazarus, Companions of Our Lord**

Gw	Isa. 25. 6–9 *or* Ps. 49. 1–10, 16 Heb. 2. 10–15 John 12. 1–8	Jer. 15. 10, 16–end Ps. 59. 1–4, 18–end Matt. 13. 44–46	Ps. 34 1 Sam. ch. 16 Luke 23. 44–56a	Ps. 119. 33–56 Jer. 33. 1–13 James ch. 3

30 Thursday **William Wilberforce, Social Reformer; Olaudah Equiano and Thomas Clarkson, Anti-Slavery Campaigners, 1833, 1797 and 1846**

Gw	Com. Saint *also* Job 31. 16–23 Gal. 3. 26–end; 4. 6–7 Luke 4. 16–21	*or* Jer. 18. 1–6 Ps. 146. 1–5 Matt. 13. 47–53	Ps. 37† 1 Sam. 17. 1–30 Luke 23.56b – 24.12	Ps. 39; ***40*** Jer. 33. 14–end James 4. 1–12

31 Friday *Ignatius of Loyola, Founder of the Society of Jesus, 1556*

G		Jer. 26. 1–9 Ps. 69. 4–10 Matt. 13. 54–end	Ps. 31 1 Sam. 17. 31–54 Luke 24. 13–35	Ps. 35 Jer. ch. 35 James 4.13 – 5.6

		Sunday Principal Service Weekday Eucharist	Third Service Morning Prayer	Second Service Evening Prayer
August 2026				
1 Saturday				
G		Jer. 26. 11–16, 24 Ps. 69. 14–20 Matt. 14. 1–12	Ps. 41; ***42***; 43 1 Sam. 17.55 – 18.16 Luke 24. 36–end	Ps. 45; ***46*** Jer. 36. 1–18 James 5. 7–end **ct**
2 Sunday	**THE NINTH SUNDAY AFTER TRINITY (Proper 13)**			
G	*Track 1* Gen. 32. 22–31 Ps. 17. 1–7, 16 (*or* 17. 1–7) Rom. 9. 1–5 Matt. 14. 13–21	*Track 2* Isa. 55. 1–5 Ps. 145. 8–9, 15–end (*or* 145. 15–end) Rom. 9. 1–5 Matt. 14. 13–21	Ps. 85 Song of Sol. 5. 2–end *or* 1 Macc. 3. 1–12 2 Pet. 1. 1–15	Ps. 80 (*or* 80. 1–8) 1 Kings 10. 1–13 Acts 13. 1–13 *Gospel*: John 6. 24–35
3 Monday				
G **DEL 18**		Jer. ch. 28 Ps. 119. 89–96 Matt. 14. 13–21 *or* 14. 22–end	Ps. 44 1 Sam. 19. 1–18 Acts 1. 1–14	Ps. ***47***; 49 Jer. 36. 19–end Mark 1. 1–13

4 Tuesday *John-Baptiste Vianney, Curé d'Ars, Spiritual Guide, 1859*

G			Jer. 30. 1–2, 12–15, 18–22 Ps. 102. 16–21 Matt. 14. 22–end *or* 15. 1–2, 10–14	Ps. ***48***; 52 1 Sam. 20. 1–17 Acts 1. 15–end	Ps. 50 Jer. ch. 37 Mark 1. 14–20

5 Wednesday **Oswald, King of Northumbria, Martyr, 642**

Gr	Com. Martyr *esp.* 1 Pet. 4. 12–end John 16. 29–end	*or*	Jer. 31. 1–7 Ps. 121 Matt. 15. 21–28	Ps. 119. 57–80 1 Sam. 20. 18–end Acts 2. 1–21	Ps. ***59***; 60; (67) Jer. 38. 1–13 Mark 1. 21–28 *or First EP of The Transfiguration* Ps. 99; 110 Exod. 24. 12–end John 12. 27–36a **𝔚 ct**

6 Thursday **THE TRANSFIGURATION OF OUR LORD**

𝔚			Dan. 7. 9–10, 13–14 Ps. 97 2 Pet. 1. 16–19 Luke 9. 28–36	*MP*: Ps. 27; 150 Ecclus. 48. 1–10 *or* 1 Kings 19. 1–16 1 John 3. 1–3	*EP*: Ps. 72 Exod. 34. 29–end 2 Cor. ch. 3

		Sunday Principal Service Weekday Eucharist	Third Service Morning Prayer	Second Service Evening Prayer
7 Friday	*John Mason Neale, Priest, Hymn Writer, 1866*			
G		Nahum 2. 1, 3; 3. 1–3, 6–7 Ps. 137. 1–6 *or* Deut. 32. 35–36, 39, 41 Matt. 16. 24–28	Ps. ***51***; 54 1 Sam. 22. 6–end Acts 2. 37–end	Ps. 38 Jer. ch. 39 Mark 2. 1–12
8 Saturday	**Dominic, Priest, Founder of the Order of Preachers, 1221**			
Gw	Com. Religious *or* *also* Ecclus. 39. 1–10	Hab. 1.12 – 2.4 Ps. 9. 7–11 Matt. 17. 14–20	Ps. 68 1 Sam. ch. 23 Acts 3. 1–10	Ps. 65; **66** Jer. ch. 40 Mark 2. 13–22 **ct**
9 Sunday	**THE TENTH SUNDAY AFTER TRINITY (Proper 14)**			
G	*Track 1* Gen. 37. 1–4, 12–28 Ps. 105. 1–6, 16–22, 45b (*or* 105. 1–10) Rom. 10. 5–15 Matt. 14. 22–33	*Track 2* 1 Kings 19. 9–18 Ps. 85. 8–13 Rom. 10. 5–15 Matt. 14. 22–33	Ps. 88 Song of Sol. 8. 5–7 *or* 1 Macc. 14. 4–15 2 Pet. 3. 8–13	Ps. 86 1 Kings 11.41 – 12.20 Acts 14. 8–20 *Gospel*: John 6. 35, 41–51

10 Monday	**Laurence, Deacon at Rome, Martyr, 258**				
Gr **DEL 19**	Com. Martyr *also* 2 Cor. 9. 6–10	*or*	Ezek. 1. 2–5, 24–end Ps. 148. 1–4, 12–13 Matt. 17. 22–end	Ps. 71 1 Sam. ch. 24 Acts 3. 11–end	Ps. ***72***; 75 Jer. ch. 41 Mark 2.23 – 3.6
11 Tuesday	**Clare of Assisi, Founder of the Minoresses (Poor Clares), 1253** *John Henry Newman, Priest, Tractarian, 1890*				
Gw	Com. Religious *esp.* Song of Sol. 8. 6–7	*or*	Ezek. 2.8 – 3.4 Ps. 119. 65–72 Matt. 18. 1–5, 10, 12–14	Ps. 73 1 Sam. ch. 26 Acts 4. 1–12	Ps. 74 Jer. ch. 42 Mark 3. 7–19a
12 Wednesday					
G			Ezek. 9. 1–7; 10. 18–22 Ps. 113 Matt. 18. 15–20	Ps. 77 1 Sam. 28. 3–end Acts 4. 13–31	Ps. 119. 81–104 Jer. ch. 43 Mark 3. 19b–end
13 Thursday	**Jeremy Taylor, Bishop of Down and Connor, Teacher, 1667** *Florence Nightingale, Nurse, Social Reformer, 1910; Octavia Hill, Social Reformer, 1912*				
Gw	Com. Teacher *also* Titus 2. 7–8, 11–14	*or*	Ezek. 12. 1–12 Ps. 78. 58–64 Matt. 18.21 – 19.1	Ps. 78. 1–39† 1 Sam. ch. 31 Acts 4.32 – 5.11	Ps. 78. 40–end† Jer. 44. 1–14 Mark 4. 1–20

August 2026		Sunday Principal Service Weekday Eucharist	Third Service Morning Prayer	Second Service Evening Prayer
14 Friday	*Maximilian Kolbe, Friar, Martyr, 1941*			
G		Ezek. 16. 1–15, 60–end Ps. 118. 14–18 *or Canticle*: Song of Deliverance Matt. 19. 3–12	Ps. 55 2 Sam. ch. 1 Acts 5. 12–26	Ps. 69 Jer. 44. 15–end Mark 4. 21–34 *or First EP of The Blessed Virgin Mary* Ps. 72 Prov. 8. 22–31 John 19. 23–27 **W ct**
15 Saturday	**THE BLESSED VIRGIN MARY***			
W		Isa. 61. 10–end *or* Rev. 11.19 - 12.6, 10 Ps. 45. 10–end Gal. 4. 4–7 Luke 1. 46–55	*MP*: Ps. 98; 138; 147. 1–12 Isa. 7. 10–15 Luke 11. 27–28	*EP*: Ps. 132 Song of Sol. 2. 1–7 Acts 1. 6–14
	or, if The Blessed Virgin Mary is celebrated on 8 September:			
G		Ezek. 18. 1–11a, 13b, 30, 32 Ps. 51. 1–3, 15–17 Matt. 19. 13–15	Ps. ***76***; 79 2 Sam. 2. 1–11 Acts 5. 27–end	Ps. 81; ***84*** Jer. ch. 45 Mark 4. 35–end **ct**

16 Sunday	**THE ELEVENTH SUNDAY AFTER TRINITY (Proper 15)**			
G	*Track 1* Gen. 45. 1–15 Ps. 133 Rom. 11. 1–2a, 29–32 Matt. 15. [10–20] 21–28	*Track 2* Isa. 56. 1, 6–8 Ps. 67 Rom. 11. 1–2a, 29–32 Matt. 15. [10–20] 21–28	Ps. 92 Jonah ch. 1 *or* Ecclus. 3. 1–15 2 Pet. 3. 14–end	Ps. 90 (*or* 90. 1–12) 2 Kings 4. 1–37 Acts 16. 1–15 *Gospel*: John 6. 51–58
17 Monday				
G **DEL 20**		Ezek. 24. 15–24 Ps. 78. 1–8 Matt. 19. 16–22	Ps. ***80***; 82 2 Sam. 3. 12–end Acts ch. 6	Ps. ***85***; 86 Mic. 1. 1–9 Mark 5. 1–20
18 Tuesday				
G		Ezek. 28. 1–10 Ps. 107. 1–3, 40, 43 Matt. 19. 23–end	Ps. 87; ***89. 1–18*** 2 Sam. 5. 1–12 Acts 7. 1–16	Ps. 89. 19–end Mic. ch. 2 Mark 5. 21–34
19 Wednesday				
G		Ezek. 34. 1–11 Ps. 23 Matt. 20. 1–16	Ps. 119. 105–128 2 Sam. 6. 1–19 Acts 7. 17–43	Ps. ***91***; 93 Mic. ch. 3 Mark 5. 35–end

*The Blessed Virgin Mary may be celebratec on 8 September instead of 15 August.

		Sunday Principal Service Weekday Eucharist	Third Service Morning Prayer	Second Service Evening Prayer
20 Thursday	**Bernard, Abbot of Clairvaux, Teacher, 1153** *William and Catherine Booth, Founders of the Salvation Army, 1912 and 1890*			
Gw	Com. Religious *or* *esp.* Rev. 19. 5–9	Ezek. 36. 23–28 Ps. 51. 7–12 Matt. 22. 1–14	Ps. 90; **92** 2 Sam. 7. 1–17 Acts 7. 44–53	Ps. 94 Mic. 4.1 – 5.1 Mark 6. 1–13
21 Friday				
G		Ezek. 37. 1–14 Ps. 107. 1–8 Matt. 22. 34–40	Ps. ***88***; (95) 2 Sam. 7. 18–end Acts 7.54 – 8.3	Ps. 102 Mic. 5. 2–end Mark 6. 14–29
22 Saturday				
G		Ezek. 43. 1–7 Ps. 85. 7–end Matt. 23. 1–12	Ps. 96; ***97***; 100 2 Sam. ch. 9 Acts 8. 4–25	Ps. 104 Mic. ch. 6 Mark 6. 30–44 **ct**

23 Sunday	**THE TWELFTH SUNDAY AFTER TRINITY (Proper 16)**			
G	*Track 1* Exod. 1.8 – 2.10 Ps. 124 Rom. 12. 1–8 Matt. 16. 13–20	*Track 2* Isa. 51. 1–6 Ps. 138 Rom. 12. 1–8 Matt. 16. 13–20	Ps. 104. 1–25 Jonah ch. 2 *or* Ecclus. 3. 17–29 Rev. ch. 1	Ps. 95 2 Kings 6. 8–23 Acts 17. 15–end *Gospel*: John 6. 56–69 *or First EP of Bartholomew* Ps. 97 Isa. 61. 1–9 2 Cor. 6. 1–10 **R ct**
24 Monday	**BARTHOLOMEW THE APOSTLE**			
R **DEL 21**		Isa. 43. 8–13 *or* Acts 5. 12–16 Ps. 145. 1–7 Acts 5. 12–16 *or* 1 Cor. 4. 9–15 Luke 22. 24–30	*MP*: Ps. 86; 117 Gen. 28. 10–17 John 1. 43–end	*EP*: Ps. 91; 116 Ecclus. 39. 1–10 *or* Deut. 18. 15–19 Matt. 10. 1–22
25 Tuesday				
G		2 Thess. 2. 1–3a, 14–end Ps. 98 Matt. 23. 23–26	Ps. 106† (*or* Ps. 103) 2 Sam. 12. 1–25 Acts 9. 1–19a	Ps. 107† Mic. 7. 8–end Mark 7. 1–13

August/ September 2026			Sunday Principal Service Weekday Eucharist	Third Service Morning Prayer	Second Service Evening Prayer
26 Wednesday					
G			2 Thess. 3. 6–10, 16–end Ps. 128 Matt. 23. 27–32	Ps. 110; ***111***; 112 2 Sam. 15. 1–12 Acts 9. 19b–31	Ps. 119. 129–152 Hab. 1. 1–11 Mark 7. 14–23
27 Thursday	**Monica, Mother of Augustine of Hippo, 387**				
Gw	Com. Saint *also* Ecclus. 26. 1–3, 13–16	*or*	1 Cor. 1. 1–9 Ps. 145. 1–7 Matt. 24. 42–end	Ps. 113; ***115*** 2 Sam. 15. 13–end Acts 9. 32–end	Ps. 114; ***116***; 117 Hab. 1.12 – 2.5 Mark 7. 24–30
28 Friday	**Augustine, Bishop of Hippo, Teacher, 430**				
Gw	Com. Teacher *esp.* Ecclus. 39. 1–10 *also* Rom. 13. 11–13	*or*	1 Cor. 1. 17–25 Ps. 33. 6–12 Matt. 25. 1–13	Ps. 139 2 Sam. 16. 1–14 Acts 10. 1–16	Ps. ***130***; 131; 137 Hab. 2. 6–end Mark 7. 31–end
29 Saturday	**The Beheading of John the Baptist**				
Gr	Jer. 1. 4–10 Ps. 11 Heb. 11.32 – 12.2 Matt. 14. 1–12	*or*	1 Cor. 1. 26–end Ps. 33. 12–15, 20–end Matt. 25. 14–30	Ps. 120; ***121***; 122 2 Sam. 17. 1–23 Acts 10. 17–33	Ps. 118 Hab. 3. 2–19a Mark 8. 1–10 **ct**

30 Sunday	**THE THIRTEENTH SUNDAY AFTER TRINITY (Proper 17)**			
G	*Track 1* Exod. 3. 1–15 Ps. 105. 1–6, 23–26, 45b *or* Ps. 115 Rom. 12. 9–end Matt. 16. 21–end	*Track 2* Jer. 15. 15–21 Ps. 26. 1–8 Rom. 12. 9–end Matt. 16. 21–end	Ps. 107. 1–32 Jonah 3. 1–9 *or* Ecclus. 11. 7–28 (*or* 19–28) Rev. 3. 14–end	Ps. 105. 1–15 2 Kings 6. 24–25; 7. 3–end Acts 18. 1–16 *Gospel*: Mark 7. 1–8, 14–15, 21–23
31 Monday	**Aidan, Bishop of Lindisfarne, Missionary, 651**			
Gw **DEL 22**	Com. Missionary *also* 1 Cor. 9. 16–19 *or*	1 Cor. 2. 1–5 Ps. 33. 12–21 Luke 4. 16–30	Ps. 123; 124; 125; ***126*** 2 Sam. 18. 1–18 Acts 10. 34–end	Ps. ***127***; 128; 129 Hag. 1. 1–11 Mark 8. 11–21

September 2026

1 Tuesday	*Giles of Provence, Hermit, c. 710*			
G		1 Cor. 2. 10b–end Ps. 145. 10–17 Luke 4. 31–37	Ps. ***132***; 133 2 Sam. 18.19 – 19.8a Acts 11. 1–18	Ps. (134); ***135*** Hag. 1.12 – 2.9 Mark 8. 22–26

September 2026		Sunday Principal Service Weekday Eucharist	Third Service Morning Prayer	Second Service Evening Prayer
2 Wednesday	*The Martyrs of Papua New Guinea, 1901 and 1942*			
G		1 Cor. 3. 1–9 Ps. 62 Luke 4. 38–end	Ps. 119. 153–end 2 Sam. 19. 8b–23 Acts 11. 19–end	Ps. 136 Hag. 2. 10–end Mark 8.27 – 9.1
3 Thursday	**Gregory the Great, Bishop of Rome, Teacher, 604**			
Gw	Com. Teacher *or* *also* 1 Thess. 2. 3–8	1 Cor. 3. 18–end Ps. 24. 1–6 Luke 5. 1–11	Ps. ***143***; 146 2 Sam. 19. 24–end Acts 12. 1–17	Ps. ***138***; 140; 141 Zech. 1. 1–17 Mark 9. 2–13
4 Friday	*Birinus, Bishop of Dorchester (Oxon), Apostle of Wessex, 650**			
G		1 Cor. 4. 1–5 Ps. 37. 3–8 Luke 5. 33–end	Ps. 142; ***144*** 2 Sam. 23. 1–7 Acts 12. 18–end	Ps. 145 Zech. 1.18 – 2.end Mark 9. 14–29
5 Saturday				
G		1 Cor. 4. 6–15 Ps. 145. 18–end Luke 6. 1–5	Ps. 147 2 Sam. ch. 24 Acts 13. 1–12	Ps. ***148***; 149; 150 Zech. ch. 3 Mark 9. 30–37 **ct**

6 Sunday	**THE FOURTEENTH SUNDAY AFTER TRINITY (Proper 18)**			
G	*Track 1* Exod. 12. 1–14 Ps. 149 Rom. 13. 8–end Matt. 18. 15–20	*Track 2* Ezek. 33. 7–11 Ps. 119. 33–40 Rom. 13. 8–end Matt. 18. 15–20	Ps. 119. 17–32 Jonah 3.10 – 4.11 *or* Ecclus. 27.30 – 28.9 Rev. 8. 1–5	Ps. 108; [115] Ezek. 12.21 – 13.16 Acts 19. 1–20 *Gospel*: Mark 7. 24–end
7 Monday				
G **DEL 23**		1 Cor. 5. 1–8 Ps. 5. 5–9a Luke 6. 6–11	Ps. ***1***; 2; 3 1 Kings 1. 5–31 Acts 13. 13–43	Ps. ***4***; 7 Zech. ch. 4 Mark 9. 38–end
8 Tuesday	**The Birth of the Blessed Virgin Mary**** (The Accession of King Charles III may be observed on 8 September, and Collect, Readings and Post-Communion for the sovereign used.)			
Gw	Com. BVM *or*	1 Cor. 6. 1–11 Ps. 149. 1–5 Luke 6. 12–19	Ps. ***5***; 6; (8) 1 Kings 1.32 – 2.4, 10–12 Acts 13.44 – 14.7	Ps. ***9***; 10† Zech. 6. 9–end Mark 10. 1–16

*Cuthbert may be celebrated on 4 September instead of 20 March.
**The Blessed Virgin Mary may be celebrated on 8 September instead of 15 August.

September 2026		Sunday Principal Service Weekday Eucharist	Third Service Morning Prayer	Second Service Evening Prayer
9 Wednesday	*Charles Fuge Lowder, Priest, 1880*			
G		1 Cor. 7. 25–31 Ps. 45. 11–end Luke 6. 20–26	Ps. 119. 1–32 1 Kings ch. 3 Acts 14. 8–end	Ps. ***11***; 12; 13 Zech. ch. 7 Mark 10. 17–31
10 Thursday				
G		1 Cor. 8. 1–7, 11–end Ps. 139. 1–9 Luke 6. 27–38	Ps. 14; ***15***; 16 1 Kings 4.29 – 5.12 Acts 15. 1–21	Ps. 18† Zech. 8. 1–8 Mark 10. 32–34
11 Friday				
G		1 Cor. 9. 16–19, 22–end Ps. 84. 1–6 Luke 6. 39–42	Ps. 17; ***19*** 1 Kings 6. 1, 11–28 Acts 15. 22–35	Ps. 22 Zech. 8. 9–end Mark 10. 35–45
12 Saturday				
G		1 Cor. 10. 14–22 Ps. 116. 10–end Luke 6. 43–end	Ps. 20; 21; ***23*** 1 Kings 8. 1–30 Acts 15.36 – 16.5	Ps. ***24***; 25 Zech. 9. 1–12 Mark 10. 46–end **ct**

13 Sunday	**THE FIFTEENTH SUNDAY AFTER TRINITY (Proper 19)**			
G	*Track 1* Exod. 14. 19–end Ps. 114 *or Canticle*: Exod. 15. 1b–11, 20–21 Rom. 14. 1–12 Matt. 18. 21–35	*Track 2* Gen. 50. 15–21 Ps. 103. 1–13 (*or* 103. 8–13) Rom. 14. 1–12 Matt. 18. 21–35	Ps. 119. 65–88 Isa. 44.24 – 45.8 Rev. 12. 1–12	Ps. 119. 41–48 [49–64] Ezek. 20. 1–8, 33–44 Acts 20. 17–end *Gospel*: Mark 8. 27–end *or First EP of Holy Cross Day* Ps. 66 Isa. 52.13 – 53.end Eph. 2. 11–end **R ct**
14 Monday	**HOLY CROSS DAY**			
R **DEL 24**		Num. 21. 4–9 Ps. 22. 23–28 Phil. 2. 6–11 John 3. 13–17	*MP*: Ps. 2; 8; 146 Gen. 3. 1–15 John 12. 27–36a	*EP*: Ps. 110; 150 Isa. 63. 1–16 1 Cor. 1. 18–25
15 Tuesday	**Cyprian, Bishop of Carthage, Martyr, 258**			
Gr	Com. Martyr *esp.* 1 Pet. 4. 12–end *also* Matt. 18. 18–22	*or* 1 Cor. 12. 12–14, 27–end Ps. 100 Luke 7. 11–17	Ps. 32; **36** 1 Kings 8.63 – 9.9 Acts 16. 25–end	Ps. 33 Zech. 11. 4–end Mark 11. 12–26

September 2026			Sunday Principal Service Weekday Eucharist	Third Service Morning Prayer	Second Service Evening Prayer
16 Wednesday	**Ninian, Bishop of Galloway, Apostle of the Picts, c. 432** *Edward Bouverie Pusey, Priest, Tractarian, 1882*				
Gw	Com. Missionary *esp.* Acts 13. 46–49 Mark 16. 15–end	*or*	1 Cor. 12.13b – 13.end Ps. 33. 1–12 Luke 7. 31–35	Ps. 34 1 Kings 10. 1–25 Acts 17. 1–15	Ps. 119. 33–56 Zech. 12. 1–10 Mark 11. 27–end
17 Thursday	**Hildegard, Abbess of Bingen, Visionary, 1179**				
Gw	Com. Religious *also* 1 Cor. 2. 9–13 Luke 10. 21–24	*or*	1 Cor. 15. 1–11 Ps. 118. 1–2, 17–20 Luke 7. 36–end	Ps. 37† 1 Kings 11. 1–13 Acts 17. 16–end	Ps. 39; ***40*** Zech. ch. 13 Mark 12. 1–12
18 Friday					
G			1 Cor. 15. 12–20 Ps. 17. 1–8 Luke 8. 1–3	Ps. 31 1 Kings 11. 26–end Acts 18. 1–21	Ps. 35 Zech. 14. 1–11 Mark 12. 13–17
19 Saturday	*Theodore of Tarsus, Archbishop of Canterbury, 690*				
G			1 Cor. 15. 35–37, 42–49 Ps. 30. 1–5 Luke 8. 4–15	Ps. 41; ***42***; 43 1 Kings 12. 1–24 Acts 18.22 – 19.7	Ps. 45; ***46*** Zech. 14. 12–end Mark 12. 18–27 **ct**

20 Sunday	**THE SIXTEENTH SUNDAY AFTER TRINITY (Proper 20)**			
G	*Track 1* Exod. 16. 2–15 Ps. 105. 1–6, 37–end (*or* 105. 37–end) Phil. 1. 21–enc Matt. 20. 1–16	*Track 2* Jonah 3.10 – 4.end Ps. 145. 1–8 Phil. 1. 21–end Matt. 20. 1–16	Ps. 119. 153–end Isa. 45. 9–22 Rev. 14. 1–5	Ps. 119. 113–136 (*or* 119. 121–128) Ezek. 33.23, 30 – 34.10 Acts 26. 1, 9–25 *Gospel*: Mark 9. 30–37 *or First EP of Matthew* Ps. 34 Isa. 33. 13–17 Matt. 6. 19–end **R ct**
21 Monday	**MATTHEW, APOSTLE AND EVANGELIST**			
R **DEL 25**		Prov. 3. 13–18 Ps. 119. 65–72 2 Cor. 4. 1–6 Matt. 9. 9–13	*MP*: Ps. 49; 117 1 Kings 19. 15–end 2 Tim. 3. 14–end	*EP*: Ps. 119. 33–40, 89–96 Eccles. 5. 4–12 Matt. 19. 16–end
22 Tuesday				
G		Prov. 21. 1–6, 10–13 Ps. 119. 1–8 Luke 8. 19–21	Ps. ***48***; 52 1 Kings 13. 11–end Acts 19. 21–end	Ps. 50 Ecclus. 1. 11–end *or* Ezek. 1.15 – 2.2 Mark 12. 35–end

September 2026		Sunday Principal Service Weekday Eucharist	Third Service Morning Prayer	Second Service Evening Prayer
23 Wednesday	Ember Day			
G *or* **R**		Prov. 30. 5–9 Ps. 119. 105–112 Luke 9. 1–6	Ps. 119. 57–80 1 Kings ch. 17 Acts 20. 1–16	Ps. ***59***; 60; (67) Ecclus. ch. 2 *or* Ezek. 2.3 – 3.11 Mark 13. 1–13
24 Thursday				
G		Eccles. 1. 2–11 Ps. 90. 1–6 Luke 9. 7–9	Ps. 56; ***57***; (63†) 1 Kings 18. 1–20 Acts 20. 17–end	Ps. 61; ***62***; 64 Ecclus. 3. 17–29 *or* Ezek. 3. 12–end Mark 13. 14–23
25 Friday	**Lancelot Andrewes, Bishop of Winchester, Spiritual Writer, 1626** Ember Day *Sergei of Radonezh, Russian Monastic Reformer, Teacher, 1392*			
Gw *or* **Rw**	Com. Bishop *esp.* Isa. 6. 1–8 *or*	Eccles. 3. 1–11 Ps. 144. 1–4 Luke 9. 18–22	Ps. ***51***; 54 1 Kings 18. 21–end Acts 21. 1–16	Ps. 38 Ecclus. 4. 11–28 *or* Ezek. ch. 8 Mark 13. 24–31

26 Saturday	Ember Day* *Wilson Carlile, Founder of the Church Army, 1942*			
G *or* **R**		Eccles. 11.9 – 12.8 Ps. 90. 1–2, 12–end Luke 9. 43b–45	Ps. 68 1 Kings ch. 19 Acts 21. 17–36	Ps. 65; **66** Ecclus. 4.29 – 6.1 *or* Ezek. ch. 9 Mark 13. 32–end **ct**
27 Sunday	**THE SEVENTEENTH SUNDAY AFTER TRINITY (Proper 21)**			
G	*Track 1* Exod. 17. 1–7 Ps. 78. 1–4, 12–16 (*or* 78. 1–7) Phil. 2. 1–13 Matt. 21. 23–32	*Track 2* Ezek. 18. 1–4, 25–end Ps. 25. 1–8 Phil. 2. 1–13 Matt. 21. 23–32	Ps. 125; 126; 127 Isa. 48. 12–21 Luke 11. 37–54	Ps. [120; 123]; 124 Ezek. 37. 15–end 1 John 2. 22–end *Gospel*: Mark 9. 38–end

September/ October 2026		Sunday Principal Service Weekday Eucharist	Third Service Morning Prayer	Second Service Evening Prayer
28 Monday				
G **DEL 26**		Job 1. 6–end Ps. 17. 1–11 Luke 9. 46–50	Ps. 71 1 Kings ch. 21 Acts 21.37 – 22.21	Ps. **72**; 75 Ecclus. 6. 14–end *or* Ezek. 10. 1–19 Mark 14. 1–11 *or First EP of Michael and All Angels* Ps. 91 2 Kings 6. 8–17 Matt. 18. 1–6, 10 **W ct**
29 Tuesday	**MICHAEL AND ALL ANGELS**			
W		Gen. 28. 10–17 *or* Rev. 12. 7–12 Ps. 103. 19–end Rev. 12. 7–12 *or* Heb. 1. 5–end John 1. 47–end	*MP*: Ps. 34; 150 Tobit 12. 6–end *or* Dan. 12. 1–4 Acts 12. 1–11	*EP*: Ps. 138; 148 Dan. 10. 4–end Rev. ch. 5

30 Wednesday *Jerome, Translator of the Scriptures, Teacher, 420*

G	Job 9. 1–12, 14–16 Ps. 88. 1–6, 11 Luke 9. 57–end	Ps. 77 1 Kings 22. 29–45 Acts 23. 12–end	Ps. 119. 81–104 Ecclus. 10. 6–8, 12–24 *or* Ezek. 12. 1–16 Mark 14. 26–42

October 2026

1 Thursday *Remigius, Bishop of Rheims, Apostle of the Franks, 533; Anthony Ashley Cooper, Earl of Shaftesbury, Social Reformer, 1885*

G	Job 19. 21–27a Ps. 27. 13–16 Luke 10. 1–12	Ps. 78. 1–39† 2 Kings 1. 2–17 Acts 24. 1–23	Ps. 78. 40–end† Ecclus. 11. 7–28 *or* Ezek. 12. 17–end Mark 14. 43–52

2 Friday

G	Job 38. 1, 12–21; 40. 3–5 Ps. 139. 6–11 Luke 10. 13–16	Ps. 55 2 Kings 2. 1–18 Acts 24.24 – 25.12	Ps. 69 Ecclus. 14.20 – 15.10 *or* Ezek. 13. 1–16 Mark 14. 53–65

October 2026		Sunday Principal Service Weekday Eucharist	Third Service Morning Prayer	Second Service Evening Prayer
3 Saturday	*George Bell, Bishop of Chichester, Ecumenist, Peacemaker, 1958*			
G		Job 42. 1–3, 6, 12–end Ps. 119. 169–end Luke 10. 17–24	Ps. ***76***; 79 2 Kings 4. 1–37 Acts 25. 13–end	Ps. 81; ***84*** Ecclus. 15. 11–end *or* Ezek. 14. 1–11 Mark 14. 66–end **ct** *or First EP of Dedication Festival* Ps. 24 2 Chron. 7. 11–16 John 4. 19–29 **W ct**
4 Sunday	**THE EIGHTEENTH SUNDAY AFTER TRINITY (Proper 22)**			
G	*Track 1* Exod. 20. 1–4, 7–9, 12–20 Ps. 19 (*or* 19. 7–end) Phil. 3. 4b–14 Matt. 21. 33–end	*Track 2* Isa. 5. 1–7 Ps. 80. 9–17 Phil. 3. 4b–14 Matt. 21. 33–end	Ps. 128; 129; 134 Isa. 49. 13–23 Luke 12. 1–12	Ps. 136 (*or* 136. 1–9) Prov. 2. 1–11 1 John 2. 1–17 *Gospel*: Mark 10. 2–16

or, if observed as Dedication Festival:

𝔚		1 Kings 8. 22–30 *or* Rev. 21. 9–14 Ps. 122 Heb. 12. 18–24 Matt. 21. 12–16	*MP*: Ps. 48; 150 Hag. 2. 6–9 Heb. 10. 19–25	*EP*: Ps. 132 Jer. 7. 1–11 1 Cor. 3. 9–17 *Gospel*: Luke 19. 1–10
5 Monday				
G **DEL 27**		Gal. 1. 6–12 Ps. 111. 1–6 Luke 10. 25–37	Ps. ***80***; 82 2 Kings ch. 5 Acts 26. 1–23	Ps. ***85***; 86 Ecclus. 16. 17–end *or* Ezek. 14. 12–end Mark 15. 1–15
6 Tuesday	**William Tyndale, Translator of the Scriptures, Reformation Martyr, 1536**			
Gr	Com. Martyr *also* Prov. 8. 4–11 2 Tim. 3. 12–end	*or* Gal. 1. 13–end Ps. 139. 1–9 Luke 10. 38–end	Ps. 87; ***89. 1–18*** 2 Kings 6. 1–23 Acts 26. 24–end	Ps. 89. 19–end Ecclus. 17. 1–24 *or* Ezek. 18. 1–20 Mark 15. 16–32
7 Wednesday				
G		Gal. 2. 1–2, 7–14 Ps. 117 Luke 11. 1–4	Ps. 119. 105–128 2 Kings 9. 1–16 Acts 27. 1–26	Ps. ***91***; 93 Ecclus. 18. 1–14 *or* Ezek. 18. 21–32 Mark 15. 33–41

October 2026		Sunday Principal Service Weekday Eucharist	Third Service Morning Prayer	Second Service Evening Prayer
8 Thursday				
G		Gal. 3. 1–5 *Canticle*: Benedictus Luke 11. 5–13	Ps. 90; **92** 2 Kings 9. 17–end Acts 27. 27–end	Ps. 94 Ecclus. 19. 4–17 *or* Ezek. 20. 1–20 Mark 15. 42–end
9 Friday	*Denys, Bishop of Paris, and his Companions, Martyrs, c. 250; Robert Grosseteste, Bishop of Lincoln, Philosopher, Scientist, 1253*			
G		Gal. 3. 7–14 Ps. 111. 4–end Luke 11. 15–26	Ps. ***88***; (95) 2 Kings 12. 1–19 Acts 28. 1–16	Ps. 102 Ecclus. 19. 20–end *or* Ezek. 20. 21–38 Mark 16. 1–8
10 Saturday	**Paulinus, Bishop of York, Missionary, 644** *Thomas Traherne, Poet, Spiritual Writer, 1674*			
Gw	Com. Missionary *esp.* Matt. 28. 16–end *or*	Gal. 3. 22–end Ps. 105. 1–7 Luke 11. 27–28	Ps. 96; ***97***; 100 2 Kings 17. 1–23 Acts 28. 17–end	Ps. 104 Ecclus. 21. 1–17 *or* Ezek. 24. 15–end Mark 16. 9–end **ct**

11 Sunday	**THE NINETEENTH SUNDAY AFTER TRINITY (Proper 23)**			
G	*Track 1* Exod. 32. 1–14 Ps. 106. 1–6, 19–23 (*or* 106. 1–6) Phil. 4. 1–9 Matt. 22. 1–14	*Track 2* Isa. 25. 1–9 Ps. 23 Phil. 4. 1–9 Matt. 22. 1–14	Ps. 138; 141 Isa. 50. 4–10 Luke 13. 22–30	Ps. 139. 1–18 (*or* 139. 1–11) Prov. 3. 1–18 1 John 3. 1–15 *Gospel*: Mark 10. 17–31
12 Monday	**Wilfrid of Ripon, Bishop, Missionary, 709** *Elizabeth Fry, Prison Reformer, 1845; Edith Cavell, Nurse, 1915*			
Gw **DEL 28**	Com. Missionary *esp.* Luke 5. 1–11 *also* 1 Cor. 1. 18–25	*or* Gal. 4. 21–24, 26–27, 31; 5. 1 Ps. 113 Luke 11. 29–32	Ps. ***98***; 99; 101 2 Kings 17. 24–end Phil. 1. 1–11	Ps. ***105***† (*or* 103) Ecclus. 22. 6–22 *or* Ezek. 28. 1–19 John 13. 1–11
13 Tuesday	**Edward the Confessor, King of England, 1066**			
Gw	Com. Saint *also* 2 Sam. 23. 1–5 1 John 4. 13–16	*or* Gal. 5. 1–6 Ps. 119. 41–48 Luke 11. 37–41	Ps. ***106***†; (*or* 103) 2 Kings 18. 1–12 Phil. 1. 12–end	Ps. 107† Ecclus. 22.27 – 23.15 *or* Ezek. 33. 1–20 John 13. 12–20

		Sunday Principal Service Weekday Eucharist	Third Service Morning Prayer	Second Service Evening Prayer
14 Wednesday				
G		Gal. 5. 18–end Ps. 1 Luke 11. 42–46	Ps. 110; ***111***; 112 2 Kings 18. 13–end Phil. 2. 1–13	Ps. 119. 129–152 Ecclus. 24. 1–22 *or* Ezek. 33. 21–end John 13. 21–30
15 Thursday	**Teresa of Avila, Teacher, 1582**			
Gw	Com. Teacher *also* Rom. 8. 22–27 *or*	Eph. 1. 1–10 Ps. 98. 1–4 Luke 11. 47–end	Ps. 113; ***115*** 2 Kings 19. 1–19 Phil. 2. 14–end	Ps. 114; ***116***; 117 Ecclus. 24. 23–end *or* Ezek. 34. 1–16 John 13. 31–end
16 Friday	*Nicholas Ridley, Bishop of London, and Hugh Latimer, Bishop of Worcester, Reformation Martyrs, 1555*			
G		Eph. 1. 11–14 Ps. 33. 1–6, 12 Luke 12. 1–7	Ps. 139 2 Kings 19. 20–36 Phil. 3.1 – 4.1	Ps. ***130***; 131; 137 Ecclus. 27.30 – 28.9 *or* Ezek. 34. 17–end John 14. 1–14

17 Saturday	**Ignatius, Bishop of Antioch, Martyr, c. 107**			
Gr	Com. Martyr *also* Phil. 3. 7–12 John 6. 52–58	*or* Eph. 1. 15–end Ps. 8 Luke 12. 8–12	Ps. 120; ***121***; 122 2 Kings ch. 20 Phil. 4. 2–end	Ps. 118 Ecclus. 28. 14–end *or* Ezek. 36. 16–36 John 14. 15–end **ct** *or First EP of Luke* Ps. 33 Hos. 6. 1–3 2 Tim. 3. 10–end **R ct**
18 Sunday	**LUKE THE EVANGELIST** (or transferred to 19 October)			
R		Isa. 35. 3–6 *or* Acts 16. 6–12a Ps. 147. 1–7 2 Tim. 4. 5–17 Luke 10. 1–9	*MP*: Ps. 145; 146 Isa. ch. 55 Luke 1. 1–4	*EP*: Ps. 103 Ecclus. 38. 1–14 *or* Isa. 61. 1–6 Col. 4. 7–end
	or, for The Twentieth Sunday after Trinity (Proper 24):			
G	*Track 1* Exod. 33. 12–end Ps. 99 1 Thess. 1. 1–10 Matt. 22. 15–22	*Track 2* Isa. 45. 1–7 Ps. 96. 1–9 [10–13] 1 Thess. 1. 1–10 Matt. 22. 15–22	Ps. 145; 149 Isa. 54. 1–14 Luke 13. 31–end	Ps. 142 [143. 1–11] Prov. 4. 1–18 1 John 3.16 – 4.6 *Gospel*: Mark 10. 35–45

		Sunday Principal Service Weekday Eucharist	Third Service Morning Prayer	Second Service Evening Prayer
19 Monday	**Henry Martyn, Translator of the Scriptures, Missionary in India and Persia, 1812**			
Gw **DEL 29**	Com. Missionary *esp.* Mark 16. 15–end *also* Isa. 55. 6–11 *or*	Eph. 2. 1–10 Ps. 100 Luke 12. 13–21	Ps. 123; 124; 125; ***126*** 2 Kings 21. 1–18 1 Tim. 1. 1–17	Ps. ***127***; 128; 129 Ecclus. 31. 1–11 *or* Ezek. 37. 1–14 John 15. 1–11
20 Tuesday				
G		Eph. 2. 12–end Ps. 85. 7–end Luke 12. 35–38	Ps. ***132***; 133 2 Kings 22.1 – 22.3 1 Tim. 1.18 – 2.end	Ps. (134); ***135*** Ecclus. 34. 9–end *or* Ezek. 37. 15–end John 15. 12–17
21 Wednesday				
G		Eph. 3. 2–12 Ps. 98 Luke 12. 39–48	Ps. 119. 153–end 2 Kings 23. 4–25 1 Tim. ch. 3	Ps. 136 Ecclus. ch. 35 *or* Ezek. 39. 21–end John 15. 18–end

22 Thursday			
G	Eph. 3. 14–end Ps. 33. 1–6 Luke 12. 49–53	Ps. ***143***; 146 2 Kings 23.36 – 24.17 1 Tim. ch. 4	Ps. ***138***; 140; 141 Ecclus. 37. 7–24 *or* Ezek. 43. 1–12 John 16. 1–15
23 Friday			
G	Eph. 4. 1–6 Ps. 24. 1–6 Luke 12. 54–end	Ps. 142; ***144*** 2 Kings 24.18 – 25.12 1 Tim. 5. 1–16	Ps. 145 Ecclus. 38. 1–14 *or* Ezek. 44. 4–16 John 16. 16–22
24 Saturday			
G	Eph. 4. 7–16 Ps. 122 Luke 13. 1–9	Ps. 147 2 Kings 25. 22–end 1 Tim. 5. 17–end	Ps. ***148***; 149; 150 Ecclus. 38. 24–end *or* Ezek. 47. 1–12 John 16. 23–end **ct**

October 2026		Sunday Principal Service Weekday Eucharist	Third Service Morning Prayer	Second Service Evening Prayer
25 Sunday	**THE LAST SUNDAY AFTER TRINITY (Proper 25)***			
G	*Track 1* Deut. 34. 1–12 Ps. 90. 1–6, 13–end (*or* 90. 1–6) 1 Thess. 2. 1–8 Matt. 22. 34–end	*Track 2* Lev. 19. 1–2, 15–18 Ps. 1 1 Thess. 2. 1–8 Matt. 22. 34–end	Ps. 119. 137–152 Isa. 59. 9–20 Luke 14. 1–14	Ps. 119. 89–104 Eccles. chs 11 and 12 2 Tim. 2. 1–7 *Gospel*: Mark 12. 28–34
	or, if being observed as Bible Sunday:			
G		Neh. 8. 1–4a [5–6] 8–12 Ps. 119. 9–16 Col. 3. 12–17 Matt. 24. 30–35	Ps. 119. 137–152 Deut. 17. 14–15, 18–end John 5. 36b–end	Ps. 119. 89–104 Isa. 55. 1–11 Luke 4. 14–30
26 Monday	**Alfred the Great, King of the West Saxons, Scholar, 899** *Cedd, Abbot of Lastingham, Bishop of the East Saxons, 664***			
Gw **DEL 30**	Com. Saint *also* 2 Sam. 23. 1–5 John 18. 33–37	*or* Eph. 4.32 – 5.8 Ps. 1 Luke 13. 10–17	Ps. ***1***; 2; 3 Judith ch. 4 *or* Exod. 22. 21–27; 23. 1–17 1 Tim. 6. 1–10	Ps. ***4***; 7 Ecclus. 39. 1–11 *or* Eccles. ch. 1 John 17. 1–5

Day	Colour / Commemoration		Principal Service	Morning Prayer	Evening Prayer
27 Tuesday					
G			Eph. 5. 21–end Ps. 128 Luke 13. 18–21	Ps. ***5***; 6; (8) Judith 5.1 – 6.4 *or* Exod. 29.38 – 30.16 1 Tim. 6. 11–end	Ps. **9**; 10† Ecclus. 39. 13–end *or* Eccles. ch. 2 John 17. 6–19 *or First EP of Simon and Jude* Ps. 124; 125; 126 Deut. 32. 1–4 John 14. 15–26 **R ct**
28 Wednesday	**SIMON AND JUDE, APOSTLES**				
R			Isa. 28. 14–16 Ps. 119. 89–96 Eph. 2. 19–end John 15. 17–end	*MP*: Ps. 116; 117 Wisd. 5. 1–16 *or* Isa. 45. 18–end Luke 6. 12–16	*EP*: Ps. 119. 1–16 1 Macc. 2. 42–66 *or* Jer. 3. 11–18 Jude 1–4, 17–end
29 Thursday	**James Hannington, Bishop of Eastern Equatorial Africa, Martyr in Uganda, 1885**				
Gr	Com. Martyr *esp.* Matt. 10. 28–39	*or*	Eph. 6. 10–20 Ps. 144. 1–2, 9–11 Luke 13. 31–end	Ps. 14; ***15***; 16 Judith 7. 19–end *or* Lev. ch. 9 2 Tim. 1.15 – 2.13	Ps. 18† Ecclus. 43. 1–12 *or* Eccles. 3.16 – 4.end John 18. 1–11

*If the Dedication Festival is kept on this Sunday, use the provision given on 3 and 4 October.
**Chad may be celebrated with Cedd on 26 October instead of 2 March.

		Sunday Principal Service Weekday Eucharist	Third Service Morning Prayer	Second Service Evening Prayer
30 Friday				
G		Phil. 1. 1–11 Ps. 111 Luke 14. 1–6	Ps. 17; ***19*** Judith 8. 9–end *or* Lev. 16. 2–24 2 Tim. 2. 14–end	Ps. 22 Ecclus. 43. 13–end *or* Eccles. ch. 5 John 18. 12–27
31 Saturday	*Martin Luther, Reformer, 1546*			
G		Phil. 1. 18–26 Ps. 42. 1–7 Luke 14. 1, 7–11	Ps. 20; 21; ***23*** Judith ch. 9 *or* Lev. ch. 17 2 Tim. ch. 3	*First EP of All Saints* Ps. 1; 5 Ecclus. 44. 1–15 *or* Isa. 40. 27–end Rev. 19. 6–10 **𝔚 ct**

November 2026

1 Sunday	**ALL SAINTS' DAY**			
𝔚		Rev. 7. 9–end Ps. 34. 1–10 1 John 3. 1–3 Matt. 5. 1–12	*MP*: Ps. 15; 84; 149 Isa. ch. 35 Luke 9. 18–27	*EP*: Ps. 148; 150 Isa. 65. 17–end Heb. 11.32 – 12.2

2 Monday	**Commemoration of the Faithful Departed (All Souls' Day)**				
Rp *or* **Gp** **DEL 31**	Lam. 3. 17–26, 31–33 *or* Wisd. 3. 1–9 Ps. 23 *or* Ps. 27. 1–6, 16–end Rom. 5. 5–11 *or* 1 Pet. 1. 3–9 John 5. 19–25 *or* John 6. 37–40	*or*	Phil. 2. 1–4 Ps. 131 Luke 14. 12–14	Ps. **2**; 146 *alt.* Ps. 27; ***30*** Dan. ch. 1 Rev. ch. 1	Ps. **92**; 96; 97 *alt.* Ps. 26; **28**; 29 Isa. 1. 1–20 Matt. 1. 18–end
3 Tuesday	**Richard Hooker, Priest, Anglican Apologist, Teacher, 1600** *Martin of Porres, Friar, 1639*				
Rw *or* **Gw**	Com. Teacher *esp.* John 16. 12–15 *also* Ecclus. 44. 10–15	*or*	Phil. 2. 5–11 Ps. 22. 22–27 Luke 14. 15–24	Ps. ***5***; 147. 1–12 *alt.* Ps. 32; ***36*** Dan. 2. 1–24 Rev. 2. 1–11	Ps. 98; 99; ***100*** *alt.* Ps. 33 Isa. 1. 21–end Matt. 2. 1–15
4 Wednesday					
R *or* **G**			Phil. 2. 12–18 Ps. 27. 1–5 Luke 14. 25–33	Ps. ***9***; 147. 13–end *alt.* Ps. 34 Dan. 2. 25–end Rev. 2. 12–end	Ps. 111; ***112***; 116 *alt.* Ps. 119. 33–56 Isa. 2. 1–11 Matt. 2. 16–end

November 2026		Sunday Principal Service Weekday Eucharist	Third Service Morning Prayer	Second Service Evening Prayer
5 Thursday				
R *or* **G**		Phil. 3. 3–8a Ps. 105. 1–7 Luke 15. 1–10	Ps. 11; ***15***; 148 *alt*. Ps. 37† Dan. 3. 1–18 Rev. 3. 1–13	Ps. 118 *alt*. Ps. 39; ***40*** Isa. 2. 12–end Matt. ch. 3
6 Friday	*Leonard, Hermit, 6th century; William Temple, Archbishop of Canterbury, Teacher, 1944*			
R *or* **G**		Phil. 3.17 – 4.1 Ps. 122 Luke 16. 1–8	Ps. ***16***; 149 *alt*. Ps. 31 Dan. 3. 19–end Rev. 3. 14–end	Ps. 137; 138; ***143*** *alt*. Ps. 35 Isa. 3. 1–15 Matt. 4. 1–11
7 Saturday	**Willibrord of York, Bishop, Apostle of Frisia, 739**			
Rw *or* **Gw**	Com. Missionary *esp*. Isa. 52. 7–10 Matt. 28. 16–end *or*	Phil. 4. 10–19 Ps. 112 Luke 16. 9–15	Ps. ***18. 31–end***; 150 *alt*. Ps. 41; ***42***; 43 Dan. 4. 1–18 Rev. ch. 4	Ps. 145 *alt*. Ps. 45; ***46*** Isa. 4.2 – 5.7 Matt. 4. 12–22 **ct**

8 Sunday	**THE THIRD SUNDAY BEFORE ADVENT** (Remembrance Sunday)				
R *or* **G**	Wisd. 6. 12–16 *Canticle*: Wisd. 6. 17–20 1 Thess. 4. 13–end Matt. 25. 1–13	*or*	Amos 5. 18–24 Ps. 70 1 Thess. 4. 13–end Matt. 25. 1–13	Ps. 91 Deut. 17. 14–end 1 Tim. 2. 1–7	Ps. [20]; 82 Judg. 7. 2–22 John 15. 9–17
9 Monday	*Margery Kempe, Mystic, c. 1440*				
R *or* **G** **DEL 32**			Titus 1. 1–9 Ps. 24. 1–6 Luke 17. 1–6	Ps. 19; ***20*** *alt*. Ps. 44 Dan. 4. 19–end Rev. ch. 5	Ps. 34 *alt*. Ps. ***47***; 49 Isa. 5. 8–24 Matt. 4.23 – 5.12
10 Tuesday	**Leo the Great, Bishop of Rome, Teacher, 461**				
Rw *or* **Gw**	Com. Teacher *also* 1 Pet. 5. 1–11	*or*	Titus 2. 1–8, 11–14 Ps. 37. 3–5, 30–32 Luke 17. 7–10	Ps. ***21***; 24 *alt*. Ps. ***48***; 52 Dan. 5. 1–12 Rev. ch. 6	Ps. 36; ***40*** *alt*. Ps. 50 Isa. 5. 25–end Matt. 5. 13–20

November 2026			Sunday Principal Service Weekday Eucharist	Third Service Morning Prayer	Second Service Evening Prayer
11 Wednesday	**Martin, Bishop of Tours, c. 397**				
Rw *or* **Gw**	Com. Bishop *also* 1 Thess. 5. 1–11 Matt. 25. 34–40	*or*	Titus 3. 1–7 Ps. 23 Luke 17. 11–19	Ps. ***23***; 25 *alt.* Ps. 119. 57–80 Dan. 5. 13–end Rev. 7. 1–4, 9–end	Ps. 37 *alt.* Ps. ***59***; 60; (67) Isa. ch. 6 Matt. 5. 21–37
12 Thursday					
R *or* **G**			Philemon 7–20 Ps. 146. 4–end Luke 17. 20–25	Ps. ***26***; 27 *alt.* Ps. 56; ***57***; (63†) Dan. ch. 6 Rev. ch. 8	Ps. 42; ***43*** *alt.* Ps. 61; ***62***; 64 Isa. 7. 1–17 Matt. 5. 38–end
13 Friday	**Charles Simeon, Priest, Evangelical Divine, 1836**				
Rw *or* **Gw**	Com. Pastor *esp.* Mal. 2. 5–7 *also* Col. 1. 3–8 Luke 8. 4–8	*or*	2 John 4–9 Ps. 119. 1–8 Luke 17. 26–end	Ps. 28; ***32*** *alt.* Ps. ***51***; 54 Dan. 7. 1–14 Rev. 9. 1–12	Ps. 31 *alt.* Ps. 38 Isa. 8. 1–15 Matt. 6. 1–18

14 Saturday	*Samuel Seabury, first Anglican Bishop in North America, 1796*				
R *or* **G**			3 John 5–8 Ps. 112 Luke 18. 1–8	Ps. 33 *alt.* Ps. 68 Dan. 7. 15–end Rev. 9. 13–end	Ps. 84; ***86*** *alt.* Ps. 65; ***66*** Isa. 8.16 – 9.7 Matt. 6. 19–end **ct**
15 Sunday	**THE SECOND SUNDAY BEFORE ADVENT**				
R *or* **G**			Zeph. 1. 7, 12–end Ps. 90. 1–8 [9–11] 12 (*or* 90. 1–8) 1 Thess. 5. 1–11 Matt. 25. 14–30	Ps. 98 Dan. 10. 19–end Rev. ch. 4	Ps. 89. 19–37 (*or* 89. 19–29) 1 Kings 1. 15–40 (*or* 1–40) Rev. 1. 4–18 *Gospel*: Luke 9. 1–6
16 Monday	**Margaret, Queen of Scotland, Philanthropist, Reformer of the Church, 1093** *Edmund Rich of Abingdon, Archbishop of Canterbury, 1240*				
Rw *or* **Gw** **DEL 33**	Com. Saint *also* Prov. 31. 10–12, 20, 26–end 1 Cor. 12.13 – 13.3 Matt. 25. 34–end	*or*	Rev. 1. 1–4; 2. 1–5 Ps. 1 Luke 18. 35–end	Ps. 46; ***47*** *alt.* Ps. 71 Dan. 8. 1–14 Rev. ch. 10	Ps. 70; ***71*** *alt.* Ps. ***72***; 75 Isa. 9.8 – 10.4 Matt. 7. 1–12

November 2026			Sunday Principal Service Weekday Eucharist	Third Service Morning Prayer	Second Service Evening Prayer
17 Tuesday	**Hugh, Bishop of Lincoln, 1200**				
Rw *or* **Gw**	Com. Bishop *also* 1 Tim. 6. 11–16	*or*	Rev. 3. 1–6, 14–end Ps. 15 Luke 19. 1–10	Ps. 48; ***52*** *alt*. Ps. 73 Dan. 8. 15–end Rev. 11. 1–14	Ps. ***67***; 72 *alt*. Ps. 74 Isa. 10. 5–19 Matt. 7. 13–end
18 Wednesday	**Elizabeth of Hungary, Princess of Thuringia, Philanthropist, 1231**				
Rw *or* **Gw**	Com. Saint *esp*. Matt. 25. 31–end *also* Prov. 31. 10–end	*or*	Rev. ch. 4 Ps. 150 Luke 19. 11–28	Ps. ***56***; 57 *alt*. Ps. 77 Dan. 9. 1–19 Rev. 11. 15–end	Ps. 73 *alt*. Ps. 119. 81–104 Isa. 10. 20–32 Matt. 8. 1–13
19 Thursday	**Hilda, Abbess of Whitby, 680** *Mechtild, Béguine of Magdeburg, Mystic, 1280*				
Rw *or* **Gw**	Com. Religious *esp*. Isa. 61.10 – 62.5	*or*	Rev. 5. 1–10 Ps. 149. 1–5 Luke 19. 41–44	Ps. 61; ***62*** *alt*. Ps. 78. 1–39† Dan. 9. 20–end Rev. ch. 12	Ps. 74; ***76*** *alt*. Ps. 78. 40–end† Isa. 10.33 – 11.9 Matt. 8. 14–22

20 Friday	**Edmund, King of the East Angles, Martyr, 870** *Priscilla Lydia Sellon, a Restorer of the Religious Life in the Church of England, 1876*				
R *or* **Gr**	Com. Martyr *also* Prov. 20. 28; 21. 1–4, 7	*or*	Rev. 10. 8–end Ps. 119. 65–72 Luke 19. 45–end	Ps. ***63***; 65 *alt.* Ps. 55 Dan. 10.1 – 11.1 Rev. 13. 1–10	Ps. 77 *alt.* Ps. 69 Isa. 11.10 – 12.end Matt. 8. 23–end
21 Saturday					
R *or* **G**			Rev. 11. 4–12 Ps. 144. 1–9 Luke 20. 27–40	Ps. 78. 1–39 *alt.* Ps. ***76***; 79 Dan. ch. 12 Rev. 13. 11–end	Ps. 78. 40–end *alt.* Ps. 81; ***84*** Isa. 13. 1–13 Matt. 9. 1–17 **ct** *or First EP of Christ the King* Ps. 99; 100 Isa. 10.33 – 11.9 1 Tim. 6. 11–16 **R** *or* **W ct**

November 2026		Sunday Principal Service Weekday Eucharist	Third Service Morning Prayer	Second Service Evening Prayer
22 Sunday	**CHRIST THE KING** The Sunday Next Before Advent			
R *or* **W**		Ezek. 34. 11–16, 20–24 Ps. 95. 1–7 Eph. 1. 15–end Matt. 25. 31–end	*MP*: Ps. 29; 110 Isa. 4.2 – 5.7 Luke 19. 29–38	*EP*: Ps. 93; [97] 2 Sam. 23. 1–7 *or* 1 Macc. 2. 15–29 Matt. 28. 16–end
23 Monday	**Clement, Bishop of Rome, Martyr, c. 100**			
R *or* **Gr** **DEL 34**	Com. Martyr *also* Phil. 3.17 – 4.3 Matt. 16. 13–19 *or*	Rev. 14. 1–5 Ps. 24. 1–6 Luke 21. 1–4	Ps. 92; ***96*** *alt*. Ps. ***80***; 82 Isa. 40. 1–11 Rev. 14. 1–13	Ps. ***80***; 81 *alt*. Ps. ***85***; 86 Isa. 14. 3–20 Matt. 9. 18–34
24 Tuesday				
R *or* **G**		Rev. 14. 14–19 Ps. 96 Luke 21. 5–11	Ps. ***97***; 98; 100 *alt*. Ps. 87; ***89. 1–18*** Isa. 40. 12–26 Rev. 14.14 – 15.end	Ps. 99; ***101*** *alt*. Ps. 89. 19–end Isa. ch. 17 Matt. 9.35 – 10.15

25 Wednesday *Catherine of Alexandria, Martyr, 4th century; Isaac Watts, Hymn Writer, 1748*

R *or* **G**	Rev. 15. 1–4 Ps. 98 Luke 21. 12–19	Ps. 110; 111; ***112*** *alt*. Ps. 119. 105–128 Isa. 40.27 – 41.7 Rev. 16. 1–11	Ps. 121; ***122***; 123; 124 *alt*. Ps. ***91***; 93 Isa. ch. 19 Matt. 10. 16–33

26 Thursday

R *or* **G**	Rev. 18. 1–2, 21–23; 19. 1–3, 9 Ps. 100 Luke 21. 20–28	Ps. ***125***; 126; 127; 128 *alt*. Ps. 90; **92** Isa. 41. 8–20 Rev. 16. 12–end	Ps. 131; 132; ***133*** *alt*. Ps. 94 Isa. 21. 1–12 Matt. 10.34 – 11.1

27 Friday

R *or* **G**	Rev. 20.1–4, 11 – 21.2 Ps. 84. 1–6 Luke 21. 29–33	Ps. 139 *alt*. Ps. ***88***; (95) Isa. 41.21 – 42.9 Rev. ch. 17	Ps. ***146***; 147 *alt*. Ps. 102 Isa. 22. 1–14 Matt. 11. 2–19

November/ December 2026		Sunday Principal Service Weekday Eucharist	Third Service Morning Prayer	Second Service Evening Prayer
28 Saturday				
R *or* **G**		Rev. 22. 1–7 Ps. 95. 1–7 Luke 21. 34–36	Ps. 145 *alt.* Ps. 96; **97**; 100 Isa. 42. 10–17 Rev. ch. 18	Ps. 148; 149; ***150*** *alt.* Ps. 104 Isa. ch. 24 Matt. 11. 20–end **P ct**
29 Sunday	**THE FIRST SUNDAY OF ADVENT** CW Year B begins			
P		Isa. 64. 1–9 Ps. 80. 1–8, 18–20 (*or* 80. 1–8) 1 Cor. 1. 3–9 Mark 13. 24–end	Ps. 44 Isa. 2. 1–5 Luke 12. 35–48	Ps. 25 (*or* 25. 1–9) Isa. 1. 1–20 Matt. 21. 1–13 *or First EP of Andrew the Apostle* Ps. 48 Isa. 49. 1–9a 1 Cor. 4. 9–16 **R ct**

30 Monday **ANDREW THE APOSTLE**

R	Isa. 52. 7–10 Ps. 19. 1–6 Rom. 10. 12–18 Matt. 4. 18–22	*MP*: Ps. 47; 147. 1–12 Ezek. 47. 1–12 *or* Ecclus. 14. 20–end John 12. 20–32	*EP*: Ps. 87; 96 Zech. 8. 20–end John 1. 35–42

December 2026

1 Tuesday *Charles de Foucauld, Hermit in the Sahara, 1916*
Daily Eucharistic Lectionary Year 1 begins

P	Isa. 11. 1–10 Ps. 72. 1–4, 18–19 Luke 10. 21–24	Ps. ***80***; 82 *alt*. Ps. ***5***; 6; (8) Isa. 43. 1–13 Rev. ch. 20	Ps. ***74***; 75 *alt*. Ps. ***9***; 10† Isa. 26. 1–13 Matt. 12. 22–37

2 Wednesday

P	Isa. 25. 6–10a Ps. 23 Matt. 15. 29–37	Ps. 5; ***7*** *alt*. Ps. 119. 1–32 Isa. 43. 14–end Rev. 21. 1–8	Ps. 76; ***77*** *alt*. Ps. ***11***; 12; 13 Isa. 28. 1–13 Matt. 12. 38–end

December 2026		Sunday Principal Service Weekday Eucharist	Third Service Morning Prayer	Second Service Evening Prayer
3 Thursday	*Francis Xavier, Missionary, Apostle of the Indies, 1552*			
P		Isa. 26. 1–6 Ps. 118. 18–27a Matt. 7. 21, 24–27	Ps. ***42***; 43 *alt*. Ps. 14; ***15***; 16 Isa. 44. 1–8 Rev. 21. 9–21	Ps. ***40***; 46 *alt*. Ps. 18† Isa. 28. 14–end Matt. 13. 1–23
4 Friday	*John of Damascus, Monk, Teacher, c. 749; Nicholas Ferrar, Deacon, Founder of the Little Gidding Community, 1637*			
P		Isa. 29. 17–end Ps. 27. 1–4, 16–17 Matt. 9. 27–31	Ps. ***25***; 26 *alt*. Ps. 17; ***19*** Isa. 44. 9–23 Rev. 21.22 - 22.5	Ps. 16; ***17*** *alt*. Ps. 22 Isa. 29. 1–14 Matt. 13. 24–43
5 Saturday				
P		Isa. 30. 19–21, 23–26 Ps. 146. 4–9 Matt. 9.35 - 10.1, 6–8	Ps. ***9***; (10) *alt*. Ps. 20; 21; ***23*** Isa. 44.24 - 45.13 Rev. 22. 6–end	Ps. ***27***; 28 *alt*. Ps. ***24***; 25 Isa. 29. 15–end Matt. 13. 44–end **ct**

6 Sunday	**THE SECOND SUNDAY OF ADVENT**				
P			Isa. 40. 1–11 Ps. 85. 1–2, 8–end (*or* 85. 8–end) 2 Pet. 3. 8–15a Mark 1. 1–8	Ps. 80 Baruch 5. 1–9 *or* Zeph. 3. 14–end Luke 1. 5–20	Ps. 40 (*or* 40. 12–end) 1 Kings 22. 1–28 Rom. 15. 4–13 *Gospel*: Matt. 11. 2–11
7 Monday	**Ambrose, Bishop of Milan, Teacher, 397**				
Pw	Com. Teacher *also* Isa. 41. 9b–13 Luke 22. 24–30	*or*	Isa. ch. 35 Ps. 85. 7–end Luke 5. 17–26	Ps. 44 *alt*. Ps. 27; ***30*** Isa. 45. 14–end 1 Thess. ch. 1	Ps. ***144***; 146 *alt*. Ps. 26; **28**; 29 Isa. 30. 1–18 Matt. 14. 1–12
8 Tuesday	**The Conception of the Blessed Virgin Mary**				
Pw	Com. BVM	*or*	Isa. 40. 1–11 Ps. 96. 1, 10–end Matt. 18. 12–14	Ps. ***56***; 57 *alt*. Ps. 32; **36** Isa. ch. 46 1 Thess. 2. 1–12	Ps. ***11***; 12; 13 *alt*. Ps. 33 Isa. 30. 19–end Matt. 14. 13–end

December 2026		Sunday Principal Service Weekday Eucharist	Third Service Morning Prayer	Second Service Evening Prayer
9 Wednesday	Ember Day			
P		Isa. 40. 25–end Ps. 103. 8–13 Matt. 11. 28–end	Ps. ***62***; 63 *alt*. Ps. 34 Isa. ch. 47 1 Thess. 2. 13–end	Ps. ***10***; 14 *alt*. Ps. 119. 33–56 Isa. ch. 31 Matt. 15. 1–20
10 Thursday				
P		Isa. 41. 13–20 Ps. 145. 1, 8–13 Matt. 11. 11–15	Ps. 53; ***54***; 60 *alt*. Ps. 37† Isa. 48. 1–11 1 Thess. ch. 3	Ps. 73 *alt*. Ps. 39; ***40*** Isa. ch. 32 Matt. 15. 21–28
11 Friday	Ember Day			
P		Isa. 48. 17–19 Ps. 1 Matt. 11. 16–19	Ps. 85; ***86*** *alt*. Ps. 31 Isa. 48. 12–end 1 Thess. 4. 1–12	Ps. 82; ***90*** *alt*. Ps. 35 Isa. 33. 1–22 Matt. 15. 29–end

12 Saturday	Ember Day				
P			Ecclus. 48. 1–4, 9–11 *or* 2 Kings 2. 9–12 Ps. 80. 1–4, 18–19 Matt. 17. 10–13	Ps. 145 *alt*. Ps. 41; **42**; 43 Isa. 49. 1–13 1 Thess. 4. 13–end	Ps. 93; ***94*** *alt*. Ps. 45; ***46*** Isa. ch. 35 Matt. 16. 1–12 **ct**
13 Sunday	**THE THIRD SUNDAY OF ADVENT**				
P			Isa. 61. 1–4, 8–end Ps. 126 *or Canticle*: Magnificat 1 Thess. 5. 16–24 John 1. 6–8, 19–28	Ps. 50. 1–6; 62 Isa. ch. 12 Luke 1. 57–66	Ps. 68. 1–19 (*or* 68. 1–8) Mal. 3. 1–4; ch. 4 Phil. 4. 4–7 *Gospel*: Matt. 14. 1–12
14 Monday	**John of the Cross, Poet, Teacher, 1591**				
Pw	Com. Teacher *esp*. 1 Cor. 2. 1–10 *also* John 14. 18–23	*or*	Num. 24. 2–7, 15–17 Ps. 25. 3–8 Matt. 21. 23–27	Ps. 40 *alt*. Ps. 44 Isa. 49. 14–25 1 Thess. 5. 1–11	Ps. 25; ***26*** *alt*. Ps. ***47***; 49 Isa. 38. 1–8, 21–22 Matt. 16. 13–end

		Sunday Principal Service Weekday Eucharist	Third Service Morning Prayer	Second Service Evening Prayer
15 Tuesday				
P		Zeph. 3. 1–2, 9–13 Ps. 34. 1–6, 21–22 Matt. 21. 28–32	Ps. ***70***; 74 *alt.* Ps. ***48***; 52 Isa. ch. 50 1 Thess. 5. 12–end	Ps. ***50***; 54 *alt.* Ps. 50 Isa. 38. 9–20 Matt. 17. 1–13
16 Wednesday				
P		Isa. 45. 6b–8, 18, 21b–end Ps. 85. 7–end Luke 7. 18b–23	Ps. ***75***; 96 *alt.* Ps. 119. 57–80 Isa. 51. 1–8 2 Thess. ch. 1	Ps. 25; ***82*** *alt.* Ps. ***59***; 60; (67) Isa. ch. 39 Matt. 17. 14–21
17 Thursday	O Sapientia* *Eglantyne Jebb, Social Reformer, Founder of 'Save the Children', 1928*			
P		Gen. 49. 2, 8–10 Ps. 72. 1–5, 18–19 Matt. 1. 1–17	Ps. ***76***; 97 *alt.* Ps. 56; ***57***; (63†) Isa. 51. 9–16 2 Thess. ch. 2	Ps. 44 *alt.* Ps. 61; ***62***; 64 Zeph. 1.1 – 2.3 Matt. 17. 22–end

18 Friday			
P	Jer. 23. 5–8 Ps. 72. 1–2, 12–13, 18–end Matt. 1. 18–24	Ps. 77; ***98*** *alt*. Ps. ***51***; 54 Isa. 51. 17–end 2 Thess. ch. 3	Ps. 49 *alt*. Ps. 38 Zeph. 3. 1–13 Matt. 18. 1–20
19 Saturday			
P	Judg. 13. 2–7, 24–end Ps. 71. 3–8 Luke 1. 5–25	Ps. 144; ***146*** Isa. 52. 1–12 Jude	Ps. 10; ***57*** Zeph. 3. 14–end Matt. 18. 21–end **ct**
20 Sunday	**THE FOURTH SUNDAY OF ADVENT**		
P	2 Sam. 7. 1–11, 16 *Canticle*: Magnificat *or* Ps. 89. 1–4, 19–26 (*or* 1–8) Rom. 16. 25–end Luke 1. 26–38	Ps. 144 Isa. 7. 10–16 Rom. 1. 1–7	Ps. 113 [131] Zech. 2. 10–end Luke 1. 39–55

*The Evening Prayer readings from the Additional Weekday Lectionary (see p. 119) may be used from 17 to 23 December.

December 2026		Sunday Principal Service Weekday Eucharist	Third Service Morning Prayer	Second Service Evening Prayer
21 Monday*				
P		Zeph. 3. 14–18 Ps. 33. 1–4, 11–12, 20–end Luke 1. 39–45	Ps. ***121***; 122; 123 Isa. 52.13 – 53.end 2 Pet. 1. 1–15	Ps. 80; ***84*** Mal. 1. 1, 6–end Matt. 19. 1–12
22 Tuesday				
P		1 Sam. 1. 24–end Ps. 113 Luke 1. 46–56	Ps. ***124***; 125; 126; 127 Isa. ch. 54 2 Pet. 1.16 – 2.3	Ps. 24; ***48*** Mal. 2. 1–16 Matt. 19. 13–15
23 Wednesday				
P		Mal. 3. 1–4; 4. 5–end Ps. 25. 3–9 Luke 1. 57–66	Ps. 128; 129; ***130***; 131 Isa. ch. 55 2 Pet. 2. 4–end	Ps. 89. 1–37 Mal. 2.17 – 3.12 Matt. 19. 16–end
24 Thursday	**CHRISTMAS EVE**			
P		*Morning Eucharist* 2 Sam. 7. 1–5, 8–11, 16 Ps. 89. 2, 19–27 Acts 13. 16–26 Luke 1. 67–79	Ps. ***45***; 113 Isa. 56. 1–8 2 Pet. ch. 3	Ps. 85 Zech. ch. 2 Rev. 1. 1–8

25 Friday	**CHRISTMAS DAY**			
𝔴	*Any of the following sets of readings may be used on the evening of Christmas Eve and on Christmas Day. Set III should be used at some service during the celebration.*	*I* Isa. 9. 2–7 Ps. 96 Titus 2. 11–14 Luke 2. 1–14 [15–20] *II* Isa. 62. 6–end Ps. 97 Titus 3. 4–7 Luke 2. [1–7] 8–20 *III* Isa. 52. 7–10 Ps. 98 Heb. 1. 1–4 [5–12] John 1. 1–14	*MP*: Ps. ***110***; 117 Isa. 62. 1–5 Matt. 1. 18–end	*EP*: Ps. 8 Isa. 65. 17–25 Phil. 2. 5–11 *or* Luke 2. 1–20 *if it has not been used at the principal service of the day*

*Thomas the Apostle may be celebrated on 21 December instead of 3 July.

December 2026		Sunday Principal Service Weekday Eucharist	Third Service Morning Prayer	Second Service Evening Prayer
26 Saturday	**STEPHEN, DEACON, FIRST MARTYR**			
R	*The reading from Acts must be used as either the first or second reading at the Eucharist.*	2 Chron. 24. 20–22 *or* Acts 7. 51–end Ps. 119. 161–168 Acts 7. 51–end *or* Gal. 2. 16b–20 Matt. 10. 17–22	*MP*: Ps. ***13***; 31. 1–8; 150 Jer. 26. 12–15 Acts ch. 6	*EP*: Ps. 57; ***86*** Gen. 4. 1–10 Matt. 23. 34–end
27 Sunday	**JOHN, APOSTLE AND EVANGELIST** (or transferred to 29 December)			
W		Exod. 33. 7–11a Ps. 117 1 John ch. 1 John 21. 19b–end	*MP*: Ps. ***21***; 147. 13–end Exod. 33. 12–end 1 John 2. 1–11	*EP*: Ps. 97 Isa. 6. 1–8 1 John 5. 1–12
	or, for The First Sunday of Christmas:			
W		Isa. 61.10 – 62.3 Ps. 148 (*or* 148. 7–end) Gal. 4. 4–7 Luke 2. 15–21	Ps. 105. 1–11 Isa. 63. 7–9 Eph. 3. 5–12	Ps. 132 Isa. ch. 35 Col. 1. 9–20 *or* Luke 2. 41–end

28 Monday	**THE HOLY INNOCENTS**			
R		Jer. 31. 15–17 Ps. 124 1 Cor. 1. 26–29 Matt. 2. 13–18	*MP*: Ps. ***36***; 146 Baruch 4. 21–27 *or* Gen. 37. 13–20 Matt. 18. 1–10	*EP*: Ps. 123; ***128*** Isa. 49. 14–25 Mark 10. 13–16
29 Tuesday	**Thomas Becket, Archbishop of Canterbury, Martyr, 1170*** (For John, Apostle and Evangelist, see provision on 27th.)			
Wr	Com. Martyr *esp.* Matt. 10. 28–33 *also* Ecclus. 51. 1–8 *or*	1 John 2. 3–11 Ps. 96. 1–4 Luke 2. 22–35	Ps. ***19***; 20 Isa. 57. 15–end John 1. 1–18	Ps. 131; ***132*** Jonah ch. 1 Col. 1. 1–14
30 Wednesday				
W		1 John 2. 12–17 Ps. 96. 7–10 Luke 2. 36–40	Ps. 111; 112; ***113*** Isa. 59. 1–15a John 1. 19–28	Ps. ***65***; 84 Jonah ch. 2 Col. 1. 15–23

*Thomas Becket may be celebrated on 7 July instead of 29 December.

December 2026		Sunday Principal Service Weekday Eucharist	Third Service Morning Prayer	Second Service Evening Prayer
31 Thursday	*John Wyclif, Reformer, 1384*			
W		1 John 2. 18–21 Ps. 96. 1, 11–end John 1. 1–18	Ps. 102 Isa. 59. 15b–end John 1. 29–34	Ps. ***90***; 148 Jonah chs 3 & 4 Col. 1.24 – 2.7 *or First EP of The Naming of Jesus* Ps. 148 Jer. 23. 1–6 Col. 2. 8–15 **ct**

THE CHURCH OF ENGLAND

Province of Canterbury

Canterbury https://www.canterburydiocese.org

Archbishop (*Vacant*) [*Lambeth Palace, London, SE1 7JU* and *Old Palace, Canterbury, CT1 2EE*]

Suffragan Bishop – *Dover*, R. J. Hudson-Wilkin, MBE, BPhil

Dean – D. R. M. Monteith, BSc, BTh, MA, Hon. LLD

Archdeacons – *Canterbury*, W. J. Adam, BA, LLM, PhD; *Ashford*, D. N. Miller, BSocSc, BTh; *Maidstone* (*Vacant*)

Diocesan Secretary – Ian Blythe, Diocesan House, Lady Wootton's Green, Canterbury, CT1 1NQ. Tel: 01227 459401 email: iblythe@diocant.org

London https://www.london.anglican.org

Bishop – S. E. Mullally, DBE, BSc, MSc, Hon DSc [*The Old Deanery, Dean's Court, London, EC4V 5AA*] [Sarah Londin]

Area Bishops – *Kensington*, E. G. Ineson, BA, MPhil, PhD; *Willesden*, L. Nsenga-Ngoy, BA, MA; *Edmonton*, A. H. M. Jeremiah, BA, MA, MPhil, PhD; *Stepney*, J. W. Grenfell, BA, MA, DPhil

Suffragan Bishops – *Fulham*, J. M. R. Baker, BA, MPhil; *Islington*, R. C. Thorpe, BSc, BTh

Dean – A. Tremlett, BA, MA, MPhil

Archdeacons – *London*, L. J. Miller, BA, MA; *Hackney*, P. J. Farley-Moore, BA, MA; *Hampstead*, J. E. I. Hawkins, BD; *Charing Cross*, K. J. Hedderly, BA, MA; *Middlesex*, R. S. Frank; *Northolt*, C. R. Pickford, BA, MA

General Secretary – O. Home, London Diocesan House, 36 Causton Street, London, SW1P 4AU. Tel: 020 7932 1100 email: oliver.home@london.anglican.org

Collegiate Church of St Peter, Westminster

Dean – D. M. Hoyle, MBE, BA, MA, PhD, Hon. DLitt

Winchester https://winchester.anglican.org

Bishop – P. I. Mounstephen, BA, MA, PGCE [*Wolvesey, Winchester, SO23 9ND*] [Philip Winton]

Suffragan Bishops – *Southampton*, R. E. King, BA, MA; *Basingstoke* (Vacant)

Dean – (*Vacant*)

Archdeacons – *Bournemouth*, J. A. Burgess, MA; *Winchester*, R. H. G. Brand, BA, MA

Diocesan Secretary and Chief Operating Officer – C. Harbidge, Diocesan Office, Old Alresford Place, Alresford, SO24 9DH. Tel: 01962 737305 email: colin.harbidge@winchester.anglican.org

Bath and Wells https://www.bathandwells.org.uk

Bishop – N. M. R. Beasley, BSc, DPhil, BA [*The Bishop's Palace, Wells, BA5 2PD*] [Michael Bath and Wells]

Suffragan Bishop – *Taunton*, R. E. Worsley, BA, MA, LTh

Dean – T. C. Wright, BA, MA

Archdeacons – *Wells*, A. E. Gell, BA, MA, MB BS; *Bath*, C. S. Peer, BSc, PGCE, MA; *Taunton*, S. J. Hill, BA, PGCE, MA

Diocesan Secretary – Jenny Hollingsworth, Diocesan Office, Flourish House, Cathedral Park, Wells, BA5 1FD. Tel: 01749 670777

Birmingham https://cofebirmingham.com

Bishop – M. J. Volland, BA, MA, DThM [*Bishop's Croft, Old Church Road, Harborne, Birmingham, B17 0BG*] [Michael Birmingham]

Suffragan Bishop - Aston, E. T. Prior, BSc, BA, MA

Dean - M. Thompson, BA, MA, MPhil

Archdeacons - Aston, P. S. O'Hare, BA, STB, MA, PGCE; *Birmingham*, J. C. Tomlinson, BA, MA

Diocesan Secretary - J. Smart, Diocesan Office, 1 Colmore Row, Birmingham, B3 2BJ. Tel: 0121 426 0400

Bristol https://www.bristol.anglican.org

Bishop - V. F. Faull, BA, MA [*The Bishop of Bristol's Office, Church Lane, Winterbourne, Bristol, BS36 1SG*] [Vivienne Bristol]

Suffragan Bishop - Swindon, N. M. Warwick, BA

Dean - A. K. Ford, BA, MA, BTh, MA, PhD

Archdeacons - Bristol, R. A. Waring; *Malmesbury*, C. P. Bryan, BA

Diocesan Secretary - R. Leaman, Diocesan Office, First Floor, Hillside House, 1500 Parkway North, Stoke Gifford, Bristol, BS34 8YU. Tel: 0117 906 0100 email: richard.leaman@bristoldiocese.org

Chelmsford https://www.chelmsford.anglican.org

Bishop - G. E. Francis-Dehqani, BA, MA, PhD [*Bishopscourt, Main Road, Margaretting, Ingatestone, CM4 0HD*] [Guli Chelmsford]

Area Bishops - Barking, L. Cullens, BA; *Bradwell*, A. Atkinson, BA; *Colchester*, R. A. B. Morris, BSc, BA, MA, ARCS

Dean - J. H. Martin, BA, PhD

Archdeacons - Barking, C. M. Burke, LLB, MA; *Chelmsford*, J. E. Croucher, BA, MA; *Colchester*, R. J. Patten, BA, MMus; *Southend*, S. J. Lucas, BA, PGCE, MPhil, PhD, MA; *Stansted*, K. R. Peacock, BA; *West Ham*, M. A. Power

Chief Executive - M. Southworth, Diocesan Office, 53 New Street, Chelmsford, CM1 1AT. Tel: 01245 294400 email: msouthworth@chelmsford.anglican.org

Chichester https://www.chichester.anglican.org

Bishop - M. C. Warner, BA, MA, PhD [*The Palace, Chichester, PO19 1PY*] [Martin Cicestr]

Area Bishops - Horsham, R. K. F. Bushyager, MSci, BA; *Lewes*, W. P. G. Hazlewood, BA, BTh

Dean - R. E. M. Dowler, BA, PhD

Archdeacons - Chichester (*Vacant*); *Horsham*, A. F. Martin; *Hastings* (*Vacant*); *Brighton and Lewes*, M. C. Lloyd Williams, BEd

Diocesan Secretary - J. Presont, Diocesan Church House, 211 New Church Road, Hove, East Sussex, BN3 4ED. Tel: 01273 421021 email: Diocesan.Secretary@chichester.anglican.org

Coventry https://www.coventry.anglican.org

Bishop - S. R. Jelley, BA, MPhil [*Bishop's House, 23 Davenport Road, Coventry, CV5 6PW*]

Suffragan Bishop - Warwick (*Vacant*)

Dean - J. J. Witcombe, MA, MPhil

Archdeacons - Archdeacon Pastor, T. D. Cockell, BTheol (*Acting*); *Archdeacon Missioner*, B. J. Dugmore

Diocesan Secretary - J. Ladds, Cathedral and Diocesan Offices, 1 Hill Top, Coventry, CV1 5AB. Tel: 024 7652 1200 email: diocesan.secretary@coventry.anglican.org

Derby https://derby.anglican.org

Bishop - E. J. H. Lane, BA, MA [*The Bishop's Office, 6 King Street, Duffield, DE56 4EU*] [Libby Derby]

Suffragan Bishop - Repton, W. M. Macnaughton, BA

Dean - P. J. A. Robinson, BA, MA, PhD

Archdeacons - Derbyshire Peak & Dales, N. J. Fenton, BSc, BA, PGCE; *Derby City & South Derbyshire*, M. J. H. Trick, BSc, BTh; *East Derbyshire*, K. E. Hamblin, BA, PGCE

Diocesan Secretary - W. Hagger, Derby Church House, Full Street, Derby, DE1 3DR. Tel: 01332 388689 email: will.hagger@derby.anglican.org

Ely https://www.elydiocese.org

Bishop - D. Winter, DrTheol (*Acting*) [*The Bishop's House, Ely, CB7 4DW*]

Suffragan Bishop - Huntingdon, D. Winter, DrTheol

Dean - M. P. J. Bonney, BA, MA

Archdeacons - Cambridge, A. J. Hughes, BA, MA, MPhil, PhD; *Huntingdon and Wisbech*, R. J. St C. Harlow, BA, MA

Diocesan Secretary - P. L. Evans, Diocesan Office, Bishop Woodford House, Barton Road, Ely, CB7 4DX. Tel: 01353 652701 email: paul.evans@elydiocese.org

Europe (Diocese in Europe) https://www.europe.anglican.org

Bishop - R. N. Innes, BA, MA, PhD [*Office of the Bishop of Gibraltar in Europe, 47 rue Capitaine Crespel - boîte 49, 1050 Brussels, Belgium*] [Robert Gibraltar in Europe]

Suffragan Bishop in Europe - A. R. Norman, BA, MA, MPhil, AIL

Archdeacons - Eastern Europe, Germany and Northern Europe, L. Nathaniel; *France and Switzerland*, P. G. Hooper, BSc, PhD; *Gibraltar, Italy and Malta*, D. J. Waller, BA, MA, MTh; *North West Europe*, S. W. Van Leer, BA, MA

Diocesan Secretary - A. Caspari, 14 Tufton Street, London, SW1P 3QZ. Tel: 020 7898 1156 email: bron.panter@churchofengland.org

Exeter https://exeter.anglican.org

Bishop - M. R. Harrison, BA, PhD, MA [*The Palace, Exeter, EX1 1HY*] [Mike Exon]

Suffragan Bishops - Crediton (*Vacant*); *Plymouth*, J. E. Grier, BA, MA

Dean - J. D. F. Greener, BA, MA

Archdeacons - Exeter, A. M. Beane, BA; *Plymouth*, J. J. Bakker, BA; *Barnstaple*, V. Breed; *Totnes*, D. J. Dettmer, BA, MDiv

Diocesan Secretary - S. Hancock, The Old Deanery, The Cloisters, Exeter, EX1 1HS. Tel: 01392 294927 email: stephen.hancock@exeter.anglican.org

Gloucester https://www.gloucester.anglican.org

Bishop - R. Treweek, BA, BTh [*2 College Green, Gloucester, GL1 2LR*] [Rachel Gloucester]

Suffragan Bishop - Tewkesbury, R. W. Springett, BTh, MA

Dean - A. S. Zihni, BA, MA

Archdeacons - Cheltenham (*Vacant*); *Gloucester*, H. J. Dawson, BA, PGCE, MA

Diocesan Secretary - B. Preece Smith, Church House, 6 College Green, Gloucester, GL1 2LY. Tel: 01452 835523 email: bpreecesmith@glosdioc.org.uk

Guildford https://www.cofeguildford.org.uk

Bishop - A. J. Watson, BA, MA [*Willow Grange, Woking Road, Guildford, GU4 7QS*] [Andrew Guildford]

Suffragan Bishop - Dorking, R. P. Davies, BA, MTh

Dean - R. G. Cooper, BD

Archdeacons - Surrey, C. M. Mabuza, BA, MA; *Dorking*, M. C. Breadmore, LLB, BTh

Diocesan Secretary - G. Newbold, Church House, 20 Alan Turing Road, Guildford, GU2 7YF. Tel: 01483 790301 email: diocesan.secretary@cofeguildford.org.uk

Hereford https://www.hereford.anglican.org

Bishop - R. C. Jackson, BA, MSc [*The Bishop's House, The Palace, Hereford, HR4 9BN*] [Richard Hereford]

Dean - S. R. D. Brown

Archdeacons - *Hereford*, D. C. Chedzey, BA, MA; *Ludlow*, F. R. Gibson, BEd, MTh

Diocesan Secretary - S. Pratley, The Diocesan Office, The Palace, Palace Yard, Hereford, HR4 9BL. Tel: 01432 373314 email: s.pratley@hereford.anglican.org

Leicester https://www.leicester.anglican.org

Bishop - M. J. Snow, BSc, BTh [*Bishop's Lodge, 12 Springfield Road, Leicester, LE2 3BD*] [Martyn Leicester]

Suffragan Bishop - *Loughborough*, V. M. L. Muthalaly, BTh

Dean - K. S. F. Rooms, BA, MTh (*Acting*)

Archdeacons - *Leicester*, R. V. Worsfold, LLB, BA; *Loughborough*, C. Wood

Diocesan Secretary - J. W. Kerry, St Martin's House, 7 Peacock Lane, Leicester, LE1 5PZ. Tel: 0116 261 5326 email: jonathan.kerry@leicestercofe.org

Lichfield https://www.lichfield.anglican.org

Bishop - M. G. Ipgrave, OBE, BA, MA, PhD [*The Bishop's House, 22 The Close, Lichfield, WS13 7LG*] [Michael Lichfield]

Area Bishops - *Shrewsbury*, S. R. Bullock, BA; *Stafford*, M. J. Parker, BA, MA; *Wolverhampton*, T. L. Wambunya, BA

Dean - J. E. McFarlane, BMedSci, BA

Archdeacons - *Lichfield*, S. K. Weller, BSc, PhD, BA; *Salop*, J. H. Farnworth, BA, MA, and M. R. Thomas, BA, PGCE (*Acting*); *Stoke*, M. R. Smith, MBChB, MTh, MSc, MRCP, FHEA, FRCPCH; *Walsall*, J. W. Trood, BSc, PGCE and J. M. Cody, LLB, BTh (*Acting*)

Chief Executive Officer and Diocesan Secretary - (*Vacant*). Tel: 01543 306291

Lincoln https://www.lincoln.anglican.org

Bishop - S. D. Conway, BA, MA, CertEd [*Edward King House, Minster Yard, Lincoln, LN2 1PU*] [Stephen Lincoln]

Suffragan Bishops - *Grimsby*, D. E. Court, BA, BSc, PGCE, PhD; *Grantham*, N. A. Chamberlain, BA, BD, PhD

Dean - S. M. Jones, BA, MA, PhD, DPhil

Archdeacons - *Boston*, J. P. H. Allain Chapman, BA, PGCE, MDiv, DThMin, AKC; *Lincoln*, G. J. Kirk, BTh, MA, LLM; *Stow and Lindsey*, A. C. Buxton

Diocesan Secretary - Andrew Holmes, Edward King House, Minster Yard, Lincoln, LN2 1PU. Tel: 01522 504032 email: David.dadswell@lincoln.anglican.org

Norwich https://www.dioceseofnorwich.org

Bishop - G. B. Usher, BSc, BA, MA [*Bishop's House, Norwich, NR3 1SB*] [Graham Norwich]

Suffragan Bishops - *Thetford*, I. G. Bishop, BSc, MA, MRICS; *Lynn*, J. E. Steen, BA, MA, PhD, LLM

Dean - A. J. Braddock, BA, MA, PhD

Archdeacons - *Norwich*, K. N. James, BA, MA; *Lynn*, C. H. Dobson; *Norfolk*, S. J. Betts, BSc

Diocesan Secretary - T. Sweeting, Diocesan House, 109 Dereham Road, Easton, Norwich, NR9 5ES. Tel: 01603 880853 email: tim.sweeting@dioceseofnorwich.org

Oxford https://www.oxford.anglican.org

Bishop - S. J. L. Croft, BA, MA, PhD [*Church House Oxford, Langford Locks, Kidlington, Oxford, OX5 1GF*] [Steven Oxon]

Area Bishops - *Dorchester*, G. A. Collins, BA, MA; *Reading*, M. E. Gregory, BA, MA; *Buckingham*, D. T. Bull, BA

Dean of Christ Church - S. R. I. Foot, BA, MA, PhD, FSA, FRHistS

Archdeacons - *Oxford*, J. P. M. Chaffey; *Buckingham*, G. C. Elsmore, BSc; *Berkshire*, S. J. Pullin, BA, BEng, MBA; *Dorchester*, D. S. Tyler, BSc, ACA

Diocesan Secretary - M. Humphriss, Church House Oxford, Langford Locks, Kidlington, Oxford, OX5 1GF. Tel: 01865 208202 email: diocesan.secretary@oxford.anglican.org

Queen's Free Chapel of St George, Windsor Castle https://www.stgeorges-windsor.org

Dean - C. J. Cocksworth, BA, PhD, PGCE

Peterborough https://www.peterborough-diocese.org.uk

Bishop - D. M. Sellin, MA [*The Bishop's Lodging, The Palace, Peterborough, PE1 1YA*]

Suffragan Bishop - *Brixworth*, J. E. Holbrook, BA, MA

Dean - C. C. Dalliston, BA, MA

Archdeacons - *Northampton*, R. J. Ormston, BA, MTh; *Oakham*, A. S. W. Booker, BA, MA

Diocesan Secretary - A. Roberts, Diocesan Office, The Palace, Peterborough, PE1 1YB. Tel: 01733 887002 email: diosec@peterborough-diocese.org.uk

Portsmouth https://www.portsmouth.anglican.org

Bishop - J. H. Frost, BD, MTh, DUniv, MSSTh [*Bishopsgrove, 26 Osborn Road, Fareham, PO16 7DQ*] [Jonathan Portsmouth]

Dean - A. W. N. S. Cane, BA, MPhil, PhD

Archdeacons - *Portsdown*, R. C. White, BA (*Acting*); *The Meon*, K. J. Percival, BA, MA, ARCM; *Isle of Wight*, S. J. Daughtery, BSc, BA

Diocesan Secretary - P. Poulter, Diocese of Portsmouth, First Floor, Peninsular House, Wharf Road, Portsmouth, PO2 8HB. Tel: 02392 899650 email: philip.poulter@portsmouth.anglican.org

Rochester https://www.rochester.anglican.org

Bishop - J. Gibbs [*Bishopscourt, 24 St Margaret's Street, Rochester, ME1 1TS*] [Jonathan Roffen]

Suffragan Bishop - *Tonbridge*, S. D. Burton-Jones, BA, BTh, MA

Dean - P. J. Hesketh, BD, PhD, AKC

Archdeacons - *Rochester*, A. P. Davey, BA, DMinTh (*Interim*); *Tonbridge*, N. S. Cornell, BA, MA; *Bromley and Bexley*, A. Kerr

Diocesan Secretary - M. Girt, Diocesan Office, St Nicholas Church, Boley Hill, Rochester, ME1 1SL. Tel: 01634 560000 email: matthew.girt@rochester.anglican.org

St Albans https://www.stalbans.anglican.org

Bishop - A. G. C. Smith, BA, MA, PhD, HonDD [*Abbey Gate House, 4 Abbey Mill Lane, St Albans, AL3 4HD*] [Alan St Albans]

Suffragan Bishops - *Hertford*, J. Mainwaring, BA, MPhil, PhD; *Bedford*, R. W. B. Atkinson, OBE, MA

Dean - J. Kelly-Moore, BA, LLB, BD

Archdeacons - *St Albans*, C. E. C. Hudson, BA, MA; *Bedford*, D. J. Middlebrook, BA, BSc, MSc; *Hertford*, J. Mackenzie, BEd, BA

Diocesan Secretary – D. White, Diocesan Office, Holywell Lodge, 41 Holywell Hill, St Albans, AL1 1HE. Tel: 01727 818131 email: dwhite@stalbans.anglican.org

St Edmundsbury and Ipswich https://www.cofesuffolk.org

Bishop – (*Vacant*) [*The Bishop's House, 4 Park Road, Ipswich, IP1 3ST*]

Suffragan Bishop – *Dunwich* (*Vacant*)

Dean – J. P. Hawes, BA, MA

Archdeacons – *Ipswich*, R. Henderson (*Interim*); *Sudbury*, D. H. Jenkins, BA, MA, PhD; *Suffolk*, R. Henderson; *Rural Mission*, S. A. Gaze, BA, MA, MPhil, PGCE

Diocesan Secretary – G. Peverley, Diocesan Office, St Nicholas Centre, 4 Cutler Street, Ipswich, IP1 1UQ. Tel: 01473 298575 email: dbf@cofesuffolk.org

Salisbury https://www.salisbury.anglican.org

Bishop – S. D. Lake, BTh [*South Canonry, 71 The Close, Salisbury, SP1 2ER*] [Stephen Sarum]

Area Bishops – *Sherborne*, K. M. Gorham, BA; *Ramsbury*, A. P. Rumsey, BA, MA, DThMin

Dean – N. C. Papadopulos, BA, MA

Archdeacons – *Sherborne*, P. J. Sayer, BA; *Dorset*, A. C. MacRow-Wood, BA, ACA; *Sarum*, A. P. Jeans, BTh, MA, MIAAS, MIBCO; *Wilts* (*Vacant*)

Diocesan Secretary – D. Pain, Church House, Crane Street, Salisbury, SP1 2QB. Tel: 01722 411922 email: david.pain@salisbury.anglican.org

Southwark https://southwark.anglican.org

Bishop – C. T. J. Chessun, BA, MA [*Bishop's House, 38 Tooting Bec Gardens, London, SW16 1QZ*] [Christopher Southwark]

Area Bishops – *Kingston-upon-Thames*, J. M. Gainsborough, MA, MSc, PhD; *Woolwich*, A. M. Cutting, BEd, MA; *Croydon*, M. R. Mallett, BA, PhD

Dean – M. D. Oakley, BD, AKC, FKC, MA, PhD, Hon EdD

Archdeacons – *Lewisham and Greenwich*, C. Chike, BA, MTh, PhD, MA; *Southwark*, J. M. W. Sedgwick, BA, MA; *Lambeth*, S. P. Gates, MA, BA; *Wandsworth*, B. C. Shepherd, BSc, MA, BA; *Reigate*, M. A. E. Astin, BA, MA; *Croydon*, G. S. Prior, BTh

Diocesan Secretary – N. Thomas, Southwark Diocesan Office, Trinity House, 4 Chapel Court, Borough High Street, London, SE1 1HW. Tel: 020 7939 9400 email: via website

Truro https://trurodiocese.org.uk

Bishop – D. G. Williams, BSocSc [*Lis Escop, Feock, Truro, TR3 6QQ*]

Suffragan Bishop – *St Germans*, H. E. Nelson, BA

Dean – S. J. Robinson, BA

Archdeacons – *Bodmin*, K. A. Betteridge, BA, MA; *Cornwall*, C. D. Hogger, BA, LLM

Diocesan Secretary – S. P. V. Cade, BA, Church House, Woodlands Court, Truro Business Park, Threemilestone, Truro, TR4 9NH. Tel: 07517 100676 email: simon.cade@truro.anglican.org

Worcester https://www.cofe-worcester.org.uk

Bishop – M. C. W. Gorick, BA, MA (*Acting*) [*The Bishop's Office, The Old Palace, Deansway, Worcester, WR1 2JE*]

Suffragan Bishop – *Dudley*, M. C. W. Gorick, BA, MA

Dean – S. M. Edwards, BSc, MA, DPT

Archdeacons – *Worcester*, M. Badger, BTh; *Dudley*, N. J. Groarke, BA

Diocesan Secretary – A. Todd, Diocesan Office, 16 Lowesmoor Wharf, Worcester, WR1 2RS. Tel: 01905 732801 email: ATodd@cofe-worcester.org.uk

Provincial Episcopal Visitors in the Province of Canterbury
Bishop of Ebbsfleet – R. S. Munro, BSc, PGCE, BA, DMin
Bishop of Maidstone (*Vacant*)
Bishop of Oswestry – P. Thomas, BA, MA, Hon ARAM
Bishop of Richborough – L. T. Irvine-Capel, BA, MA

Province of York

York https://dioceseofyork.org.uk

Archbishop – S. G. Cottrell, BA, MA. Primate of England and Metropolitan [*Bishopthorpe Palace, York, YO23 2GE*] [Stephen Ebor]

Suffragan Bishops – *Beverley*, S. P. Race, BA, MTh; *Selby*, F. J. L. Winfield, BA, DD; *Hull*, E. R. Sanderson, BSc, MA, PhD, MTh; *Whitby*, B. L. Hill

Dean – D. M. J. Barrington, BA, MSc, LTCL, MTS, MA

Archdeacons – *York*, S. J. Rushton, BA, MA; *East Riding*, A. C. Broom, BSocSc, BA; *Cleveland*, A. E. Bloor, BA, MA, PhD, PGCE

Diocesan Secretary and Chief Executive – P. J. Warry, BSc, The Diocese of York, Amy Johnson House, Amy Johnson Way, York, YO30 4XT. Tel: 01904 699500 email: office@yorkdiocese.org

Durham https://durhamdiocese.org

Bishop – S. E. Clark, BA, MBA, MA (*Acting*) [*The Bishop of Durham's Office, Auckland Castle, Market Place, Bishop Auckland, DL14 7NR*]

Suffragan Bishop – *Jarrow*, S. E. Clark, BA, MBA, MA

Dean – P. J. J. Plyming, BA, PhD

Provost of Sunderland Minster – D. Tolhurst (*Acting*)

Archdeacons – *Sunderland* (*Vacant*); *Durham*, E. M. Wilkinson, MA; *Auckland*, R. L. Simpson, BA, MPhil, PGCE

Diocesan Secretary and Secretary to the Board of Finance – J. Morgan, Diocesan Office, Cuthbert House, Stonebridge, Durham, DH1 3RY. Tel: 07436 213127 email: james.morgan@durham.anglican.org

Blackburn https://www.blackburn.anglican.org

Bishop – P. J. North, BA, MA [*Bishop's House, Ribchester Road, Clayton-le-Dale, Blackburn, BB1 9EF*] [Philip Blackburn]

Suffragan Bishops – *Lancaster*, J. L. C. Duff, BA, MA, DPhil; *Burnley*, J. Kennedy, BSc, BD, MSt, DPhil, PGCE

Dean – P. Howell-Jones, BMus, PGCE

Archdeacons – *Blackburn*, M. C. Ireland, MTheol, MA; *Lancaster*, D. A. Picken, BA, MA, PGCE

Diocesan Secretary – S. Whittaker, Diocesan Offices, Clayton House, Walker Industrial Estate, Walker Road, Blackburn, BB1 2QE. Tel: 01254 503404 email: stephen.whittaker@blackburn.anglican.org

Carlisle https://www.carlislediocese.org.uk

Bishop – R. J. Saner-Haigh, BA, MPhil, MA (*Acting*) [*Bishop's House, Ambleside Road, Keswick, CA12 4DD*]

Suffragan Bishop – *Penrith*, R. J. Saner-Haigh, BA, MPhil, MA

Dean – J. D. Brewster, BA, MA

Archdeacons – *Carlisle*, R. E. Newton, BA, MProf, PGCE; *West Cumberland*, S. J. Fyfe, BSc; *Westmorland and Furness*, V. Ross, BSc, RGN, MA

Diocesan Secretary – D. Hurton, Church House, 19–24 Friargate, Penrith, Cumbria, CA11 7XR. Tel: 01768 807760 email: derek.hurton@carlislediocese.org.uk

Chester https://www.chester.anglican.org

Bishop - M. S. A. Tanner, BA, MA, MTh [*Bishop's House, 1 Abbey Street, Chester, CH1 2JD*] [Mark Cestr]

Suffragan Bishops - *Birkenhead*, J. A. Conalty; *Stockport*, S. J. C. Corley, BA, MA, PGCE

Dean - T. R. Stratford, BSc, PhD

Archdeacons - *Chester*, M. R. Gilbertson, BA, MA, PhD; *Macclesfield*, J. E. Proudfoot, BA, PGCE

Diocesan Secretary - C. Penn (*Interim*), Chester Diocesan Board of Finance, Church House, 5500 Daresbury Park, Daresbury, Warrington, WA4 4GE. Tel: 01928 718834 ext 247
email: chris.penn@chester.anglican.org

Leeds https://www.leeds.anglican.org

Bishop - N. Baines, BA [*Hollin House, Weetwood Avenue, Leeds, LS16 5NG*] [Nicholas Leeds]

Area Bishops - *Bradford*, T. M. Howarth, BA, MA, PhD; *Huddersfield*, M. S. Prasadam, BA, MA, LTCL; *Kirkstall*, A. Arora, LLB, BA; *Ripon*, A. Eltringham, BA; *Wakefield* (*Vacant*)

Deans - *Bradford*, A. M. Bowerman, BSc, MSW, MA; *Ripon*, J. R. Dobson, BA; *Wakefield*, S. C. Cowling, BA, MA, PGCE

Archdeacons - *Bradford*, A. J. Jolley, BSc, BTh, CEng, MIMechE, MBA, PhD; *Halifax*, W. E. Braviner, BSc, BA, MA, ACA, FCA; *Leeds*, P. N. Ayers, BA, MA; *Pontefract*, C. M. Thatcher, MA, MSc, BTh, ACCA; *Richmond and Craven*, J. W. F. Theodosius, BA, MA, DPhil, PGCE

Diocesan Secretary - J. Wood, Church House, 17-19 York Place, Leeds, LS1 2EX. Tel: 0113 353 0303 email: jonathan.wood@leeds.anglican.org

Liverpool https://liverpoolcofe.org

Bishop - J. Perumbalath, BA, BD, MA, PhD [*Bishop's Lodge, Woolton Park, Liverpool, L25 6DT*] [John Liverpool]

Suffragan Bishop - *Warrington*, B. A. Mason, BA

Dean - S. H. Jones, BEd, MPhil, PhD

Archdeacons - *Knowsley and Sefton*, P. H. Spiers, BA; *Liverpool*, M. Threlfall-Holmes, BA, MA, PhD; *St Helens and Warrington*, S. J. P. Fisher, BA; *Wigan and West Lancashire* (*Vacant*)

Diocesan Secretary - S. Parr, St James' House, 20 St James Road, Liverpool, L1 7BY. Tel: 0151 705 2112
email: mike.eastwood@liverpool.anglican.org

Manchester https://www.manchester.anglican.org

Bishop - D. S. Walker, MA, PhD [*Bishopscourt, Bury New Road, Salford, M7 4LE*] [David Manchester]

Suffragan Bishops - *Bolton*, M. J. Porter, BA, MA, DMin; *Middleton*, M. Davies, BA

Dean - R. M. Govender, MBE, BTh

Archdeacons - *Manchester*, K. B. Best; *Rochdale*, K. L. Smeeton, LLB; *Bolton and Salford*, R. Mann

Chief Operating Officer and Diocesan Secretary - H. Platts, Church House, 90 Deansgate, M3 2GH. Tel: 0161 828 1400
email: helenplatts@manchester.anglican.org

Newcastle https://www.newcastle.anglican.org

Bishop - H.-A. M. Hartley, MTheol, ThM, MPhil, DPhil [*Bishop's House, 29 Moor Road South, Gosforth, Newcastle upon Tyne, NE3 1PA*]

Suffragan Bishop - *Berwick*, M. Wroe, BA, MA

Dean - L. P. Batson, BA, MA

Archdeacons - *Lindisfarne*, C. A. Sourbut Groves, BA, MSc, PhD; *Northumberland*, R. A. Wood, BA, MA

Diocesan Secretary - C. Elder (*Interim*), Church House, St John's Terrace, North Shields, NE29 6HS. Tel: 0191 270 4114 email: diosec@newcastle.anglican.org

Sheffield https://www.sheffield.anglican.org

Bishop - P. J. Wilcox, BA, MA, DPhil [*Bishopscroft, Snaithing Lane, Sheffield, S10 3LG*] [Pete Sheffield]

Suffragan Bishop - *Doncaster* (*Vacant*)

Dean - A. L. Thompson, BMus, BA

Archdeacons - *Sheffield and Rotherham*, M. L. Chamberlain; BA, BTh, MPhil; *Doncaster*, J. Iqbal, BA, MA

Diocesan Secretary - K. Bell, Church House, 95-99 Effingham Street, Rotherham, S65 1BL. Tel: 01709 309100 email: katie.bell@sheffield.anglican.org

Sodor and Man https://www.sodorandman.im

Bishop - P. D. Hillas, BSc, BA, MSc [*Thie yn Aspick, 4 The Falls, Douglas, Isle of Man, IM4 4PZ*] [Peter Sodor and Man]

Dean - N. P. Godfrey, BA, MA, MBA, MSc

Archdeacon of Man - I. C. Cowell, RGN

Diocesan Secretary, T. Connell email: via website

Southwell and Nottingham https://southwell.anglican.org

Bishop - P. G. Williams, BA [*Bishop's Manor, Southwell, NG25 0JR*] [Paul Southwell]

Suffragan Bishop - *Sherwood*, A. N. Emerton, BSc, DPhil, BTh

Dean - N. R. Evans, MA, DMin (*Interim*)

Archdeacons - *Nottingham*, P. A. Williams, BA; *Newark*, V. C. Ramsey

Diocesan Chief Executive - M. Cooper, Jubilee House, 8 Westgate, Southwell, NG25 0JH. Tel: 01636 817206 email: ce@southwell.anglican.org

Provincial Episcopal Visitor in the Province of York

Bishop of Beverley - S. P. Race, BA, MTh [*The Bishop of Beverley's Office, Holy Trinity Rectory, Micklegate, York, YO1 6LE*] [Stephen Beverley]

The Church in Wales

St Asaph https://dioceseofstasaph.org.uk

Bishop - G. K. Cameron, BA, MA, MPhil, LLM [*Esgobty, Upper Denbigh Road, St Asaph, LL17 0TW*] [Gregory Llanelwy]

Dean - N. H. Williams

Archdeacons - *St Asaph*, A. S. Grimwood, BA, BD; *Montgomery*, G. H. Capon, BSc; *Wrexham*, H. D. Y. Matthews

Diocesan Secretary - O. Lintern-Smyth, Diocesan Office, High Street, St Asaph, Denbighshire, LL17 0RD. Tel: 01745 582245 email: olwenlinternsmyth@cinw.org.uk

Bangor https://bangor.eglwysyngnghymru.org.uk

Bishop - A. T. G. John, LLB, BA [*Tŷ'r Esgob, Upper Garth Road, Bangor, LL57 2SS*] [Andrew Bangor]

Dean (*Vacant*)

Archdeacons - *Bangor*, D. A. Parry, BSc, CQSW; *Meirionydd*, R. W. Townsend, BA, MA; *Anglesey*, J. C. Harvey, BA, BTh

Diocesan Secretary - S. R. Evans, The Diocesan Centre, Cathedral Close, Bangor, Tŷ Deiniol, LL57 1RL. Tel: 01248 354999 email: sionrhysevans@churchinwales.org.uk

Llandaff https://llandaff.churchinwales.org.uk

Bishop – M. K. R. Stallard, BA, PGCE [*Llys Esgob, The Cathedral Green, Llandaff, Cardiff, CF5 2YE*] [Mary Llandaff]

Dean – J. S. Bray

Archdeacons – *Llandaff*, R. E. A. Green, BA, MA; *Margam*, M. R. Preece, BA

Diocesan Secretary – J. Laing, The Diocesan Office, The Court, Coychurch, Bridgend, CF35 5EH. Tel: 07753 611556 email: jameslaing@churchinwales.org.uk

Monmouth https://monmouth.churchinwales.org.uk

Bishop – C. E. Vann, ARCM, GRSM [*Bishopstow, Stow Hill, Newport, NP20 4EA*] [Elizabeth Monmouth]

Dean – I. C. Black, BA, MDiv

Archdeacons – *Newport*, J. S. Williams, BSc; *Monmouth*, I. K. Rees; *Gwent Valleys*, S. Bailey, BTheol

Diocesan Secretary – I. Thompson, Monmouth Diocesan Office, 64 Caerau Road, Newport, NP20 4HJ. Tel: 01633 267490 email: isabelthompson@churchinwales.org.uk

St Davids https://stdavids.churchinwales.org.uk

Bishop – D. P. Davies, BA [*Llys Esgob, Abergwili, Carmarthen, SA31 2JG*] [Dorrien Tyddewi]

Dean – S. C. Rowland Jones, LVO, OBE, BA, MA

Archdeacons – *Carmarthen*, M. Hill; *Cardigan*, R. H. E. Davies, MBE, BTh; *St Davids*, P. R. Mackness, BA

Diocesan Secretary – H. Llewellyn, Diocesan Office, Abergwili, Carmarthen, SA31 2JG. Tel: 01267 236145 email: howardllewellyn@churchinwales.org.uk

Swansea and Brecon https://swanseaandbrecon.churchinwales.org.uk

Archbishop of Wales and Bishop of Swansea and Brecon, J. D. P. Lomas [*Ely Tower, Castle Square, Brecon, LD3 9DJ*] [John Swansea and Brecon]

Dean of Brecon Cathedral – A. P. Shakerley, MA, PhD

Archdeacons – *Brecon*, A. N. Jevons, BA, MA; *Gower*, J. B. Davies, BTh

Diocesan Secretary – L. Pearson, Diocesan Centre, Cathedral Close, Brecon, Powys, LD3 9DP. Tel: 01874 623716 email: louisepearson@churchinwales.org.uk

The Episcopal Church in Scotland

https://www.scotland.anglican.org

Aberdeen and Orkney https://aoepiscopal.scot

Bishop – A. C. Dyer, MA, MTh [*Ashley House, 16 Ashley Gardens, Aberdeen, AB10 6RQ*]

Dean (*Vacant*)

Provost of St Andrew's Cathedral, Aberdeen – I. M. Poobalan, RGN, BD, MTh, MPhil

Diocesan Secretary – E. Finlayson, The Diocese of Aberdeen and Orkney, University of Aberdeen, Marischal College, Broad Street, Aberdeen, AB10 1YS. Tel: 01224 662247 email: office@aberdeen.anglican.org

Argyll and the Isles https://argyll.anglican.org

Bishop – D. J. Railton, BPharm [*St Moluag's Diocesan Centre, Croft Avenue, Oban, PA34 5JJ*]

Dean – M. R. Campbell, BA

Provost of St John's Cathedral, Oban – M. R. Campbell, BA

Diocesan Secretary (*Vacant*), St Moluag's Diocesan Centre, Croft Avenue, Oban, PA34 5JJ. Tel: 01631 570870 email: secretary@argyll.anglican.org

Brechin https://www.thedioceseofbrechin.org

Bishop – A. C. Swift, BEng, MSc, BTh [*Bishop's House, 5 Ballumbie View, Dundee, DD4 0NQ*] [Andrew Brechin]

Dean – K. G. G. Gibson, MA, BD, PGCE

Provost of St Paul's Cathedral, Dundee – E. J. Thomson, MA, DPhil, BA, PGCE

Diocesan Secretary – J. Jacobs, Diocesan Centre, 38 Langlands Street, Dundee, DD4 6SZ. Tel: 07444 161300 email: diosec@brechin.anglican.org

Edinburgh https://edinburgh.anglican.org

Bishop – J. A. Armes, BA, MA, PhD [*Bishop's Office, 21a Grosvenor Crescent, Edinburgh, EH12 5EL*] [John Edenburgen]

Dean – F. S. Burberry, ACII

Provost of St Mary's Cathedral, Edinburgh – J. A. Conway, BEng, BD

Diocesan Secretary – W. Poon, The Diocese of Edinburgh, 21a Grosvenor Crescent, Edinburgh, EH12 5EL. Tel: 0131 538 7033 email: diosec@dioceseofedinburgh.org

Glasgow and Galloway https://www.glasgow.anglican.org

Bishop – A. C. Swift, BEng, MSc, BTh (*Acting*) [*Bishop's Office, Diocesan Centre, 5 St Vincent Place, Glasgow, G1 2DH*]

Dean – R. J. Preston, BSc, MEng, MA, PGCE

Provost of St Mary's Cathedral, Glasgow – K. Holdsworth, BSc, BD, MTh

Diocesan Secretary – J. Mitchell, Glasgow and Galloway Diocesan Centre, 5 St Vincent Place, Glasgow, G1 2DH. email: office@glasgow.anglican.org

Moray, Ross and Caithness https://www.scotland.anglican.org/who-we-are/organisation/bishops-and-their-dioceses/diocese-of-moray-ross-caithness/

Bishop, Primus of the Scottish Episcopal Church – M. J. Strange, LTh [*Bishop's House, St John's, Arpafeelie, North Kessock, Inverness, IV1 3XD*] [Mark Moray, Ross and Caithness]

Dean – S. E. Murray, BTh

Provost, St Andrew's Cathedral, Inverness – S. E. Murray, BTh

Diocesan Secretary – I. Foyers, The United Diocese of Moray, Ross and Caithness, 9–11 Kenneth Street, Inverness, IV3 5NR. Tel: 01463 237503 email: diocesansecretary@moray.anglican.org

St Andrews, Dunkeld and Dunblane https://standrews.anglican.org

Bishop – I. J. Paton, MA, PGCE, MTh [*Diocesan Office, 28a Balhousie Street, Perth, PH1 5HJ*] [Ian St Andrews]

Dean – G. S. Taylor

Provost of St Ninian's Cathedral, Perth – S. M. Holmes, MA, BD, PhD, PGCE

Diocesan Secretary (*Vacant*), The Diocese of St Andrews, Dunkeld and Dunblane, 28a Balhousie Street, Perth, PH1 5HJ. Tel: 01738 443173 email: bishopsec@standrews.anglican.org

The Church of Ireland

Province of Armagh

Armagh www.armagh.anglican.org

Archbishop – F. J. McDowell, BA, BTh, Primate of All Ireland and Metropolitan [*Church House, 46 Abbey Street, Armagh, BT61 7DZ*] [John Armagh]

Dean - T. S. Forster, BA, BTh, MPhil

Diocesan Secretary - J. Leighton, Church House, 46 Abbey Street, Armagh, BT61 7DZ. Tel: 028 3752 2858 email: secretary@armagh.anglican.org

Clogher https://clogher.anglican.org

Bishop - I. W. Ellis, BSc, CertEd, EdD, BTh [*The See House, Ballagh Road, Fivemiletown, Co. Tyrone, BT75 0QP*] [Ian Clogher]

Dean - K. R. J. Hall

Diocesan Secretary - G. M. T. Moore, Clogher Diocesan Office, St Macartin's Cathedral Hall, Halls Lane, Enniskillen, Co. Fermanagh, BT74 7DR. Tel: 028 6634 7879 email: secretary@clogher.anglican.org

Connor https://connor.anglican.org

Bishop - G. T. W. Davison, BD, BTh [*Bishop's House, 27 Grange Road, Doagh, Ballyclare, BT39 0RQ*] [George Connor]

Deans - *Connor*, W. S. Wright, BTh, MA; *Belfast*, S. Forde, BSc, DipTh

Diocesan Secretary (*Vacant*), Diocese of Connor, Channel Wharf, Unit 1, 21 Old Channel Road, Belfast, BT3 9DE. Tel: 028 9082 8830 email: office@connordiocese.org

Derry and Raphoe https://derryandraphoe.org

Bishop - A. J. Forster, BA, BTh [*Diocesan Office, 24 London Street, Londonderry, BT48 6RQ*] [Andrew Derry and Raphoe]

Deans - *Derry*, R. J. Stewart, BA, MA; *Raphoe* (*Vacant*)

Diocesan Secretary (*Vacant*), The Diocesan Office, 24 London Street, Londonderry, BT48 6RQ. Tel: 028 7126 2440 email: via website

Down and Dromore https://www.downanddromore.org

Bishop - D. A. McClay [*The See House, 32 Knockdene Park South, Belfast, BT5 7AB*] [David Down and Dromore]

Deans - *Down* (*Vacant*); *Dromore*, S. G. Wilson, BTh

Diocesan Secretary - R. Lawther, Church of Ireland House, 61-67 Donegall Street, Belfast, BT1 2QH. Tel: 028 9082 8831 email: rlawther@downdromorediocese.org

Kilmore, Elphin and Ardagh https://www.dkea.ie

Bishop - S. F. Glenfield, BA, MLitt, MA, MTh [*The See House, Kilmore Upper, Cavan, Co. Cavan, H16 TV29*] [Ferran Kilmore]

Deans - *Kilmore*, N. N. Crossey, BA; *Elphin and Ardagh*, A. Williams, BD, MA

Diocesan Secretary (*Vacant*), Diocesan Office, 20A Market Street, Cootehill, Co. Cavan, H16 XT02. Tel: 049 555 9954 email: secretary@kilmore.anglican.org

Province of Dublin

Dublin and Glendalough https://dublin.anglican.org

Archbishop - M. G. St A. Jackson, BA, MA, PhD, DPhil, Primate of Ireland and Metropolitan [*The See House, 17 Temple Road, Dartry, Dublin 6*] [Michael Dublin and Glendalough]

Dean - D. P. M. Dunne, BA, MA

Diocesan and Glebes Secretary - I. Walshe, United Dioceses of Dublin and Glendalough, Church of Ireland House, Church Avenue, Rathmines, Dublin 6, D06 CF67. Tel: 01 496 6981 email: dgsecretary@dublinchurchofireland.org

National Cathedral and Collegiate Church of St Patrick, Dublin 8 https://www.stpatrickscathedral.ie

Dean - W. W. Morton, BTh, MA, MMus, PhD

Meath and Kildare https://meathandkildare.org

Bishop - P. L. Storey, MA, BTh [*Bishop's House, Moyglare, Maynooth, Co. Kildare, W23 NK55*] [Pat Meath and Kildare]

Deans - *Clonmacnoise* (*Vacant*); *Kildare*, I. M. Jackson, BD

Diocesan Secretary - K. Seaman, Meath and Kildare Diocesan Centre, Moyglare, Maynooth, Co. Kildare, W23 WK76. Tel: 01 629 2163 email: secretary@meath.anglican.org

Cashel, Ferns and Ossory https://cashel.anglican.org

Bishop - A. M. Wilkinson, BA, MA, BTh, HDipEd [*Bishop's House, Troysgate, Kilkenny, R95 R2N1*] [Adrian Cashel Ferns and Ossory]

Deans - *Cashel*, J. G. Mulhall, DipSW, CQSW, BA; *Waterford*, B. J. Hayes; *Lismore*, P. R. Draper, BTh, MA; *Ossory (Kilkenny)*, S. A. Farrell, BA, MA, BTh, LLM; *Ferns*, P. G. Mooney, BD, ThM, DrTheol; *Leighlin* (*Vacant*)

Diocesan Secretary - E. Keyes, The Diocesan Office, The Palace Coach House, Church Lane, Kilkenny, R95 A032. Tel: 056 776 1910 email: office@cashel.anglican.org

Cork, Cloyne and Ross https://cork.anglican.org

Bishop - W. P. Colton, BCL, DipTh, MPhil, LLM, PhD [*St Nicholas House, 14 Cove Street, Cork, T12 RP40*] [Paul Cork]

Deans - *Cork*, N. K. Dunne, BA, BTh, MA, MPhil; *Cloyne*, S. D. Green, BA, HDipEd; *Ross*, C. P. Jeffers, BTh, MA

Diocesan and Glebes Secretary - J. de Montfort, The Diocesan Office, St Nicholas House, 14 Cove Street, Cork, T12 RP40. Tel: 021 500 5080 email: secretary@corkchurchofireland.com and via website

Tuam, Limerick and Killaloe https://tlk.ie

Bishop - M. A. J. Burrows, BA, MA, MLitt, DipTh [*Kilbane House, Golf Links Road, Castletroy, Limerick*] [Michael Tuam, Limerick and Killaloe]

Deans - *Tuam*, D. Matchett; *Limerick*, N. J. W. Sloane, BA, MA, MPhil; *Killaloe*, R. J. J. Marsh

Diocesan Administrator (*Tuam*) - H. Pope, 11 Ros Ard, Cappagh Road, Barna, Galway, H91 XW9A. Tel: 086 833 6666 email: secretary@tka.ie

Diocesan Secretary (*Limerick and Killaloe*) - L. Sharpe, Kellysgrove, Ballinasloe, Galway. Tel: 087 613 0063 email: diocesansecretary@limerick.anglican.org

The Churches of the Anglican Communion outside the British Isles

The Episcopal / Anglican Province of Alexandria

Archbishop of Alexandria and Bishop of Egypt - Samy Fawzy, Diocesan Office, PO Box 87, Zamalek Distribution 11211, Cairo, Egypt

The Anglican Church in Aotearoa, New Zealand and Polynesia

Primates and Archbishops - Don Tamihere, Justin Duckworth and Sione Uluilakepa, PO Box 568, Gisborne, 4040, New Zealand; Sione Uluilakepa, Box 35, Suva, Fiji; Justin Duckworth, PO Box 12-046, Wellington, 6144, New Zealand

The Anglican Church of Australia

Primate of Australia and Archbishop of Adelaide - Geoffrey Smith, 18 King William Road, North Adelaide, South Australia, 5006, Australia

Episcopal Church of Brazil (Igreja Episcopal Anglicana do Brasil)

Primate of Brazil and Bishop of Amazônia - Marinez Rosa Dos Santos Bassotto, Avenida Serzedelo Corrêa, 514 Batista Campos, Belem, PA, 66033-265, Brazil

The Anglican Church of Burundi

Archbishop of Burundi and Bishop of Buye - Sixbert Macumi, Eglise Episcopale du Burundi, BP 94, Ngozi, Burundi

The Anglican Church of Canada

Primate of the Anglican Church of Canada - Anne Germond (*Acting*), 80 Hayden Street, Toronto, Ontario, M4Y 3G2, Canada

The Church of the Province of Central Africa

Archbishop of Central Africa and Bishop of Lusaka - Albert Chama, Bishop's Lodge, PO Box 30183, Lusaka, Zambia

The Anglican Church of the Central American Region (Iglesia Anglicana de la Region Central de America)

Primate of IARCA and Bishop of El Salvador - Juan David Alvarado Melgar, 47 Avenida Sur, 723 Col Flor Blanca, Apt Postal (01), San Salvador, 274, El Salvador

Iglesia Anglicana de Chile

Primate of the Anglican Church of Chile and Diocesan Bishop of Santiago - Hector Zavala, Casilla 50675, Correo Central, Santiago, Chile

The Anglican Church of the Province of Congo (Province de L'Eglise Anglicane du Congo)

Archbishop of Congo and Bishop of Aru - Georges Titre Ande, PO Box 226, Arua, Uganda

Hong Kong Sheng Kung Hui

Archbishop and Bishop of Western Kowloon - Andrew Chan, 11 Pak Po Street, Mongkok, Kowloon, Hong Kong, People's Republic of China

The Church of the Province of the Indian Ocean

Archbishop, Province of the Indian Ocean, and Bishop of the Seychelles - James Richard Wong Yin Song, Bishop's House, Bel Eau, Victoria Mahé, Seychelles

The Nippon Sei Ko Kai (The Anglican Communion in Japan)

Primate of the NSKK and Bishop of Kyushu - David Eisho Uehara, 3-3-5 Aza Meada, Urasoe-shi, Okinawa-ken, 901-2102, Japan

The Episcopal Church in Jerusalem and the Middle East

President Bishop of the Episcopal Church in Jerusalem and the Middle East, and Anglican Archbishop in Jerusalem - Hosam Naoum, St George's Cathedral Close, Nablus Road, Box 19122, Jerusalem 91191, Israel

The Anglican Church of Kenya

Primate and Archbishop of All Kenya - Jackson Ole Sapit, PO Box 40502, Nairobi, 100, Kenya

The Anglican Church of Korea

Primate of Korea and Bishop of Busan - Onesimus Dongsin Park, Bishop's Office, Dae-Chong-Ro 99-Bon-Gil 5-1, Jung-Gu, Busan, 48933, Korea

The Anglican Church of Melanesia

Archbishop of the Anglican Church of Melanesia and Bishop of Central Melanesia - Leonard Dawea, PO Box 19, Honiara, Solomon Islands

The Mexican Episcopal Church (La Iglesia Anglicana de Mexico)

Primate and Bishop of Cuernavaca - Enrique Treviño Cruz, Minerva #1, Fracc. Delicias, Cuernavaca, Morelos, 62330, Mexico

The Anglican Church of Mozambique and Angola (Igreja Anglicana de Mocambique e Angola)

Acting Presiding Bishop of Igreja Anglicana de Mocambique e Angola and Bishop of Lebombo - Dean Augusto, Caixa Postale 120, Maputo, Mozambique

The Church of the Province of Myanmar (Burma)

Archbishop of Myanmar and Bishop of Yangon - Stephen Than Myint Oo, No. 140 Pyidaungsu Yeiktha Street, PO Box 11191, Yangon, Myanmar

The Church of Nigeria (Anglican Communion)

Metropolitan and Primate of All Nigeria and Bishop of Abuja - Henry C. Ndukuba, St Matthias House, Plot 942 Gudu District, Abuja, Nigeria

The Anglican Church of Papua New Guinea

Bishop of Aipo Rongo and Acting Archbishop of Papua New Guinea - Nathan Ingen, PO Box 893, Mount Hagen, Western Highlands Province, Papua New Guinea

The Episcopal Church in the Philippines

Prime Bishop of the Philippines - Brent Alawas, Diocesan Office, Bontoc, Mt Province, 2616, Philippines

The Episcopal Church of Rwanda (L'Eglise Episcopal au Rwanda)

Archbishop of L'Eglise Episcopal au Rwanda and Bishop of Shyira - Laurent Mbanda, EER - Shyira, PO Box 52, Ruhengeri, Rwanda

The Church of the Province of South East Asia

Bishop of Singapore and Primate of South East Asia - Titus Chung Khiam Boon, St Andrew's Village, 1 Francis Thomas Drive, #01-01, Singapore, 359340

The Anglican Church of Southern Africa

Archbishop of Cape Town and Primate of Southern Africa - Thabo Makgoba, 20 Bishopscourt Drive, Bishopscourt, Claremont, Cape Town, Western Cape, 7708, South Africa

The Anglican Church of South America

Primate of the Anglican Church of South America and Bishop of Argentina - Brian Williams, 25 de Mayo 282, Capital Federal, Buenos Aires, 1001, Argentina

The Province of the Episcopal Church of Sudan

Archbishop of the Province of Sudan and Bishop of Khartoum - Ezekiel Kumir Kondo, PO Box 65, Omdurman, Sudan

The Province of the Episcopal Church of South Sudan

Archbishop and Primate of the Province of the Episcopal Church of South Sudan and Bishop of Juba - Justin Badi Arama, Episcopal Church of South Sudan, PO Box 110, Juba, South Sudan

The Anglican Church of Tanzania

Archbishop of Tanzania and Bishop of Tanga - Maimbo Mndolwa, PO Box 35, Korogwe, Tanga, Tanzania

The Church of the Province of Uganda

Archbishop of Uganda and Bishop of Mityana - Stephen Kaziimba, PO Box 102, Mityana, Uganda

The Episcopal Church in the United States of America

Presiding Bishop - Sean Rowe, The Episcopal Church Center, 815 Second Avenue, New York, NY 10017, USA

The Church of the Province of West Africa

Primate of the CPWA and Bishop of Asante-Mampong - Cyril Kobina Ben-Smith, PO Box 220, Asante-Mampong, Ghana

The Church in the Province of the West Indies

Primate of the CPWI and Bishop of Jamaica and the Cayman Islands – Howard Gregory, Church House, 2 Caledonia Avenue, Cross Roads, Kingston 5, Jamaica

Attached to Canterbury:

The Anglican Church of Bermuda: Nicholas Dill

The Church of Ceylon: Nishantha Fernando

The Parish of the Falkland Islands: Jonathan Clark

The Lusitanian Church: Sérgio Filipe Pinho Alves

The Reformed Episcopal Church of Spain: Carlos López-Lozano

Attached to the Episcopal Church in USA: Diocese of Taiwan, the Diocese of Puerto Rico and the Diocese of Venezuela

For details of the Anglican Consultative Council, which can provide further information from the Churches of the Anglican Communion outside the British Isles, please see below.

The Anglican Consultative Council

President (*Vacant*)

Chair – Canon Margaret Swinson

Vice-Chair – Archbishop Hosam Naoum

Secretary General – The Rt Revd Anthony Poggo, the Anglican Consultative Council, the Anglican Communion Office, St Andrew's House, 16 Tavistock Crescent, London, W11 1AP. Tel: 020 7313 3903 email: secretary.general@aco.org

Anglican Centre in Rome – Director, The Rt Revd Anthony Ball, Centro Anglicano, Palazzo Doria Pamphilj, Piazza del Collegio Romano 2, 00186 Roma, Italy email: administrator@anglicancentre.it

Churches with special relations to the Anglican Communion

The following Churches are in communion with all or some provinces of the Anglican Communion:

The Church of North India (United): Moderator – The Most Revd Bijay Nayak

The Church of Bangladesh: Moderator – The Most Revd Samuel Sunil Mankhin

The Church of Pakistan (United): Moderator – The Most Rt Revd Azad Marshall

The Church of South India (United): Moderator (*Vacant*)

Mar Thoma Church (India): Metropolitan – The Most Revd Dr Theodosius Mar Thoma

Old Catholic Churches of The Union of Utrecht:

Netherlands: Archbishop of Utrecht – Bernd Wallet

Austria: Bishop – Maria Kubin

Czech Republic: Bishop – Pavel B. Stránský

Germany: Bishop – Matthias Ring

Poland: Bishop – Arthur Wiecinski

Switzerland: Bishop – Frank Bangerter

USA (Polish National Catholic Church): Prime Bishop – Anthony Mikovsky

Croatia: Bishop – Heinz Lederleitner

Philippine Independent Church: Supreme Bishop – Joel O. Porlares

The Anglican Provinces in the British Isles and Ireland are in communication with some ***Lutheran Churches:***

Finland: Archbishop of Turku and Finland - Tapio Luoma

Iceland: Bishop - Guðrún Karls Helgudóttir

Norway: Presiding Bishop - Olav Fykse Tveit

Sweden: Archbishop of Uppsala - Karin Johannesson

Estonia: Archbishop - Urmas Viilma

Lithuania: Bishop - Mindaugas Sabutis

The World Council of Churches

General Secretary - The Revd Professor Jerry Pillay, PO Box 2100, CH-1211 Geneva 2, Switzerland.

Moderator of Central Committee - Bishop Heinrich Bedford-Strohm

Ecumenical bodies

Churches Together in Britain and Ireland
https://ctbi.org.uk

General Secretary - Dr Nicola Brady, Interchurch House, 35 Lower Marsh, London, SE1 7RL. Tel: 020 3794 2288 email: info@ctbi.org.uk

Churches Together in England
https://cte.org.uk

General Secretary - Bishop Mike Royal, 27 Tavistock Square, London, WC1H 9HH. Tel: 020 7529 8131 email: mike.royal@cte.org.uk

Action of Churches Together in Scotland (ACTS)
https://www.congregational.org.uk/ecumenical-mission/acts

General Secretary - The Revd Ian Boa (*Interim*), Jubilee House, Forthside Way, Stirling, FK8 1QZ.

CYTÛN: Churches Together in Wales
https://www.cytun.co.uk

Chief Executive - The Revd Sion Brynach, Room 3.3, Hastings House, Fitzalan Court, Cardiff, CF24 0BL. Tel: 07751 446071 email: sion@cytun.cymru

Irish Council of Churches
https://www.irishchurches.org

President - The Rt Revd Sarah Groves, Inter-Church Centre, 48 Elmwood Avenue, Belfast, BT9 6AZ. Tel: 028 9066 3145 email: info@irishchurches.org

The Church of England - central structures
https://www.churchofengland.org

The General Synod of the Church of England

Church House, Great Smith Street, London, SW1P 3AZ. Tel: 020 7898 1000 email: via website (https://www.churchofengland.org/about/general-synod/contact-synod-office)

Unless otherwise indicated, all addresses in this section are as above.

Email addresses generally follow the pattern christianname.surname@churchofengland.org

Secretary General – William Nye, Tel: 020 7898 1000

Principal commissions

The Clergy Discipline Commission

Secretary Conor Gannon

The Crown Nominations Commission

Secretary Canon Stephen Knott

The Dioceses Commission

Secretary Jenny Axtell

The Faith and Order Commission

Secretary The Revd Dr Casey Strine

The Fees Advisory Commission

Secretary Katie Clarke

The Legal Advisory Commission

Secretary Adam Hobson

The Legal Aid Commission

Secretary Stephen York

The Liturgical Commission

Secretary Sue Moore

The Racial Justice Commission

Secretary Brunel James

The Archbishops' Council

(and Central Board of Finance of the Church of England)

Church House, Great Smith Street, London, SW1P 3AZ
Tel: 020 7898 1000

Unless otherwise indicated, all addresses in this section are as above.

Email addresses generally follow the pattern christianname.surname@churchofengland.org

Secretary General – William Nye, Tel: 020 7898 1000

The Appointments Committee of the Church of England

Secretary Jenny Jacobs, Tel: 020 7898 1363

Audit and Risk Committee

Secretary Muir Laurie, Tel: 020 7898 1000

Committee for Minority Ethnic Anglican Concerns

Chair The Very Revd Rogers Govender MBE

Central Secretariat

Director of Central Secretariat for the Archbishops' Council Simon Gallagher, Tel: 020 7898 1000

Clerk to the Synod Jenny Jacobs, Tel: 020 7898 1363

The Council for Christian Unity

National Advisor for Ecumenical Relations The Revd Canon Dr Jeremy Morris

Vision and Strategy

Co-Directors Debbie Clinton and Dave Male
Tel: 020 7898 1000

Communications Office

Director of Communications Hannah Howard, Tel: 020 7898 1000
Church House Publishing
Head of Publishing Dr Thomas Allain Chapman, Tel: 01603 785 925

Education and Growing Faith

Chief Education Officer The Revd Nigel Genders, Tel: 020 7898 1000

Safeguarding

Director Alexander Kubeyinje, Tel 020 7898 1000

The Legal Office

Head of the Legal Office, Chief Legal Adviser to the Archbishops' Council and the General Synod and Official Solicitor to the Church Commissioners The Revd Alexander McGregor, Tel: 020 7898 1722

Ministry Development

Director The Revd Canon Nick McKee, Tel: 020 7898 1000

Faith and Public Life

Director The Revd Dr Richard Sudworth, Tel: 020 7898 1000

Racial Justice Unit

Director The Revd Guy Hewitt
Tel: 020 7898 1000

Living in Love and Faith

Programme Director Dr Nick Shepherd
Tel: 020 7898 1000

The Church Commissioners for England

Church House, Great Smith Street, London, SW1P 3AZ
Tel: 020 7898 1000

Secretary and Chief Executive (*Vacant*)

The Three Church Estates Commissioners – Alan Smith, Marsha de Cordova, MP, (*Vacant*)

The Church of England Pensions Board

29 Great Smith Street, London, SW1P 3PS Tel: 020 7898 1000
Chief Executive John Ball

Other boards, councils, commissions, etc., of the Church of England

The Churches Conservation Trust

Chief Executive Greg Pickup, Unit 14 – c/o Vulcan Works, 34–38 Guildhall Road, Northampton, NN1 1EW. Tel: 0845 303 2760

The Corporation of the Church House

Chair Stephen Barney, Church House, 27 Great Smith Street, London, SW1P 3AZ. Tel: 020 7898 1311

Theological colleges of the Church of England

College of the Resurrection, Stocks Bank Road, Mirfield, WF14 0BW. https://college.mirfield.org.uk Tel: 01924 490441 email: alewis@mirfield.org.uk *Principal,* The Rt Revd M. C. R. Sowerby, BD, MA, AKC

Cranmer Hall (St John's College), 3 South Bailey, Durham, DH1 3RJ. https://www.cranmerhall.com Tel: 0191 334 3894 email: cranmer.admissions@durham.ac.uk *Warden,* The Revd Dr N. J. Moore, BA, MSt, DPhil

Emmanuel Theological College, 5500 Daresbury Park, Warrington WA4 4GE. https://emmanueltheologicalcollege.org.uk Tel: 01244 668571 email: info@emmanueltheologicalcollege.org.uk *Dean*, The Revd Dr M. Leyden, BA, MA, MSt, PhD

Oak Hill College, Chase Side, Southgate, London, N14 4PS. https://www.oakhill.ac.uk Tel: 020 8449 0467 email: via website *President*, The Revd Dr J. E. Robson, BA, PhD

The Queen's Foundation for Ecumenical Theological Education, Somerset Road, Edgbaston, Birmingham, B15 2QH. https://www.queens.ac.uk Tel: 0121 454 1527 email: enquire@queens.ac.uk *Principal,* The Rt Revd A. E. Hollinghurst, BA, MSt

Ridley Hall, Ridley Hall Road, Cambridge, CB3 9HG. https://www.ridley.cam.ac.uk Tel: 01223 746580 email: info@ridley.cam.ac.uk *Principal,* The Revd Prebendary Dr I. M. Hamley, BA, MA, PhD

Ripon College Cuddesdon, Cuddesdon, Oxford, OX44 9EX. https://www.rcc.ac.uk Tel: 01865 877404 email: enquiries@rcc.ac.uk *Principal*, The Rt Revd H. I. J. Southern, BA, MA

St Mellitus College, London, 24 Collingham Road, London, SW5 0LX. https://stmellitus.ac.uk Tel: 020 7052 0573 email: london@stmellitus.ac.uk *Dean*, The Revd R. J. Winfield, BA, BTh, MA

St Stephen's House, 16 Marston Street, Oxford, OX4 1JX. https://www.ssho.ac.uk Tel: 01865 599650 email: enquiries@ssho.ac.uk *Principal*, The Revd Canon Dr R. Ward, BA, MA, PhD

The Sarum Centre for Formation in Ministry, Sarum College, 19 The Close, Salisbury, SP1 2EE. www.sarum.ac.uk/ministry/ Tel: 01722 424800 email: info@sarum.ac.uk and via website *Principal*, The Revd Canon Professor J. W. Woodward, BD, AKC, STh, MPhil, PhD, FRSA

Trinity College, Stoke Hill, Stoke Bishop, Bristol, BS9 1JP. www.trinitycollegebristol.ac.uk Tel: 0117 968 2803 email: reception@trinitycollegebristol.ac.uk *Principal*, The Revd Dr S. Doherty, BA, MPhil, DPhil

Westcott House, Jesus Lane, Cambridge, CB5 8BP. https://www.westcott.cam.ac.uk Tel: 01223 741000 email: info@westcott.cam.ac.uk *Principal,* The Revd Dr H. E. Dawes, BA, MA

Wycliffe Hall, 54 Banbury Road, Oxford, OX2 6PW. https://www.wycliffe.ox.ac.uk Tel: 01865 274200 email: via website *Principal,* The Revd Dr M. F. Lloyd, BA, MA, DPhil

Theological training: part-time courses

Cuddesdon Gloucester and Hereford, 12 College Green, Gloucester, GL1 2LX. https://www.rcc.ac.uk/cuddesdon-gloucester-hereford-cgh Tel: 01452 874969 email: GloucesterHereford@rcc.ac.uk
Director, The Revd Dr. S. L. Brush, BA, MA, PhD

Eastern Region Ministry Course, ERMC, 1a The Bounds, Westminster College, Lady Margaret Road, Cambridge, CB3 0BJ. https://www.ermc.cam.ac.uk Tel: 01223 760444 email: admin@ermc.cam.ac.uk
Principal, The Revd Dr A. Jensen

Emmanuel Theological College, 5500 Daresbury Park, Warrington, WA4 4GE. https://emmanueltheologicalcollege.org.uk Tel: 01244 668571 email: info@emmanueltheologicalcollege.org.uk
Dean, The Revd Dr M. Leyden

Midlands Ministry Training Course, Midlands Gospel Partnership, c/o Stapleford Baptist Church, Stapleford, Nottingham, NG9 8DB. https://midlandsgospel.org.uk email: admin@midlandsgospel.org.uk
Director of Training, P. Hancock

Oak Hill College, Chase Side, Southgate, London, N14 4PS. https://www.oakhill.ac.uk Tel: 020 8449 0467 email: via website
President, Dr J. E. Robson, BA, PhD

Ripon College Cuddeson Part-time Pathway, Ripon College Cuddesdon, Cuddesdon, Oxford, OX44 9EX. https://www.rcc.ac.uk/cuddesdon-near-oxford Tel: 01865 877404 email: admissions@rcc.ac.uk
Director, Revd Dr S. Snyder

St Augustine's College of Theology, 52 Swan Street, West Malling, Kent, ME19 6JX. https://staugustinescollege.ac.uk Tel: 01732 252656 email: via website or admissions@staugustinescollege.ac.uk
Principal, The Revd Dr A. Gregory

St Hild College, Stocks Bank Road, Mirfield WF14 0BW. https://sthild.org Tel: 01924 481925 email: enquiries@sthild.org and via website
Principal, Dr D. McGinnis

The Sarum Centre for Formation in Ministry, Sarum College, 19 The Close, Salisbury, SP1 2EE. www.sarum.ac.uk/ministry/ Tel: 01722 424820 email: info@sarum.ac.uk
Principal, The Revd Canon Professor J. W. Woodward

South West Ministry Training Course, SWMTC, Riverside Church and Conference Centre, 13-14 Okehampton Street, St Thomas, Exeter, EX4 1DU. https://swmtc.org.uk Tel: 01392 272544 email: admin@swmtc.org.uk
Principal, The Revd Dr L. Larkin

Religious societies, institutions and publications

Further information on mission agencies may be obtained from Partnership for World Mission ***(see address on page 301)***

Additional Curates Society https://additionalcurates.co.uk
General Secretary, Fr D. Smith, Additional Curates Society, 16 Commercial Street, Birmingham, B1 1RS. Tel: 0121 382 5533 email: info@additionalcurates.co.uk

Alcuin Club https://alcuinclub.org.uk *Chairman*, The Revd Canon Dr C. Irvine, The Rectory, Route De St Andre, St Andrew, Guernsey, GY6 8XN. Tel: 01481 238568 email: alcuinclub@gmail.com

Anglican and Eastern Churches Association https://aeca.org.uk *Chairman,* The Revd Canon Dr W. Taylor, St John's Parish Office, Lansdowne Crescent, London, W11 2NN. Tel: 020 7727 4262 email: chairman@aeca.org.uk

Anglican Centre in Rome, The https://www.anglicancentreinrome.org *Development Officer UK,* c/o The Anglican Communion Office, St Andrew's House, 16 Tavistock Crescent, London, W11 1AP. Tel: 07719 534084 email: development@anglicancentre.it

Anglican Pacifist Fellowship https://www.anglicanpeacemaker.org.uk *APF Coordinator,* Sarah Maguire, 17 Short Street, Swansea, SA1 6YG. email: sarah@anglicanpeacemaker.org.uk

Anglican Society for the Welfare of Animals, The https://www.aswa.org.uk *Chair,* The Revd Dr H. Hall, PO Box 7193, Hook, Hampshire, RG27 8GT. email: secretary@angsocwelanimals.net

Association of Interchurch Families https://www.interchurchfamilies.org.uk *Executive Officer,* M. Carroll, 3rd Floor, 20 King Street, London, EC2V 8EG. Tel: 020 3384 2947 email: info@interchurchfamilies.org.uk

Baptists Together https://www.baptist.org.uk *General Secretary,* L. Green, Baptist House, PO Box 44, 129 Broadway, Didcot, OX11 8RT. Tel: 01235 517700 email: via website

Bible Reading Fellowship https://www.brf.org.uk *Chief Executive,* Canon R. Fisher, 15 The Chambers, Vineyard, Abingdon, OX14 3FE. Tel: 01865 319700 email: enquiries@brf.org.uk and via website

Bible Society https://www.biblesociety.org.uk *Chief Executive,* P. Williams, Stonehill Green, Westlea, Swindon, SN5 7DG. Tel: 01793 418222 email: via website

Boys' Brigade, The https://boys-brigade.org.uk *Chief Executive,* J. Eales, Felden Lodge, Hemel Hempstead, HP3 0BL. Tel: 0300 303 4454 email: support@boys-brigade.org.uk

Catholic Church in England and Wales, The https://www.cbcew.org.uk *General Secretary*, The Revd Canon C. Thomas, Catholic Bishops' Conference of England and Wales, 39 Eccleston Square, London, SW1V 1BX. Tel: 020 7630 8220 email: via website

CHRISM: CHRistians in Secular Ministry https://chrism.org.uk *Secretary,* M. Trivasse. Tel: 07796 366220 email: margtriv@yahoo.co.uk

Children's Society, The https://www.childrenssociety.org.uk *Chief Executive,* M. Russell, Whitecross Studios, 50 Banner Street, London, EC1Y 8ST. Tel: 0300 303 7000 email: supportercare@childrenssociety.org.uk

Christian Aid https://www.christianaid.org.uk *Chief Executive*, P. Watt, 35–41 Lower Marsh, Waterloo, London, SE1 7RL. Tel: 020 7620 4444 email: via website

Christian Evidence Society https://christianevidencesociety.org *Chair*, E. Carter. email: via website

Christians Abroad https://www.cabroad.org.uk *Chair*, A. Wileman, 399 Ringwood Road, Ferndown, Dorset, BH22 9AF. Tel: 0300 012 1201 email: support@cabroad.org.uk

Church Army https://churcharmy.org *Chief Executive Officer*, J. Davis (*Interim*), Church Army, Wilson Carlile Centre, 50 Cavendish Street, Sheffield, S3 7RZ. Tel: 0300 123 2113 email: via website

Churches Conservation Trust, The https://www.visitchurches.org.uk *Chief Executive,* G. Pickup, Unit 14 - c/o Vulcan Works, 34–38 Guildhall Road, Northampton, NN1 1EW. Tel: 020 7841 0400 email: via website

Church Lads' and Church Girls' Brigade https://www.clcgb.org.uk *Governor,* A. Hayday, St Martin's House, 2 Barnsley Road, Wath-upon-Dearne, Rotherham, S63 6PY. Tel: 01709 876535 email: contactus@clcgb.org.uk

Church Mission Society https://churchmissionsociety.org *CEO,* A. Bateman, Watlington Road, Oxford, OX4 6BZ. Tel: 01865 787400 email: via website

Church Music Society https://church-music.org.uk *Honorary Secretary,* Dr S. Lindley email: webenquiries@church-music.org.uk

Church of England Communications Office https://www.churchofengland.org/media/communications-team *Director of Communications,* H. Howard, Church House, Great Smith Street, London, SW1P 3AZ. Tel: 020 7898 1326 email: via website

Church of England Education Office, The www.churchofengland.org/about/education-and-schools/education-contacts *Chief Education Officer,* N. Genders, Church House, Great Smith Street, London, SW1P 3AZ. Tel: 020 7898 1219 email: gaylene.smith@churchofengland.org or via website

Church of England Evangelical Council https://ceec.info *Co-chairs,* The Revd L. Goddard and E. Shaw email: via website

Church of England Newspaper, The https://www.churchnewspaper.com *Editor,* A. Carey, Political and Religious Intelligence Ltd, 14 Great College Street, Westminster, London, SW1P 3RX. Tel: 020 7222 2018 email: andrew.carey@churchnewspaper.com

Church of Scotland https://churchofscotland.org.uk *Moderator,* Revd Dr S. J. Paterson, 121 George Street, Edinburgh, EH2 4YN. Tel: 0131 225 5722 email: via website

Church Pastoral Aid Society (CPAS) https://www.cpas.org.uk *Chief Executive Officer,* The Revd J. L. Scamman, Sovereign Court One (Unit 3), Sir William Lyons Road, University of Warwick Science Park, Coventry, CV4 7EZ. Tel: 0300 123 0780 email: info@cpas.org.uk and via website

Church Society https://www.churchsociety.org *Director,* The Revd Dr L. Gatiss, Ground Floor, Centre Block, Hille Business Estate, 132 St Albans Road, Watford, WD24 4AE. Tel: 01923 255410 email: via website

Church Times https://www.churchtimes.co.uk *Managing Editor,* S. Meyrick, 3rd Floor, Invicta House, 108–114 Golden Lane, London, EC1Y 0TG. Tel: 020 7776 1060 email: editor@churchtimes.co.uk

Church Urban Fund https://cuf.org.uk *Group Chief Executive Officer,* R. Wickham, The Foundry, 17 Oval Way, London, SE11 5RR. Tel: 0203 752 5655 email: hello@cuf.org.uk

Church's Ministry among Jewish People, The (CMJ UK) https://www.cmj.org.uk *Deputy Chief Executive Officer,* J. Brooks, Eagle Lodge, Hexgreave Hall Business Park, Farnsfield, Nottinghamshire, NG22 8LS. Tel: 01623 883960 email: office@cmj.org.uk and via website

Clergy Support Trust https://www.clergysupport.org.uk *Chief Executive,* The Revd B. Cahill-Nicholls, 1 Dean Trench Street, Westminster, London, SWIP 3HB. Tel: 0800 389 5192 email: via website

College of Health Care Chaplains https://www.healthcarechaplains.org *Registrar,* A. Dean, CHCC, 128 Theobald's Road, London, WC1X 8TN. Tel: 01792 703301 email: Allison.Dean@unitetheunion.org

Confraternity of The Blessed Sacrament https://confraternity.org.uk *Secretary General,* Fr P. Hutchins, c/o The ACS, 16 Commercial Street, Birmingham, B1 1RS. email: admin@confraternity.org.uk

Congregational Federation https://www.congregational.org.uk *General Secretary*, Y. Campbell, 8 Castle Gate, Nottingham, NG1 7AS. Tel: 0115 911 1460 email: via website

Council of Christians and Jews, The https://ccj.org.uk *Co-Director,* The Revd Dr N. Eddy and G. Bye, Faith House, 7 Tufton Street, London, SW1P 3QB. Tel: 020 3515 3003 email: via website

Crosslinks https://www.crosslinks.org *Mission Director,* J. McLernon, 251 Lewisham Way, London, SE4 1XF. Tel: 020 8691 6111 email: info@crosslinks.org

Ecclesiastical Insurance Group https://www.ecclesiastical.com *Managing Director UK*, R. Coleman, Benefact House, 2000 Pioneer Avenue, Gloucester Business Park, Brockworth, Gloucester, GL3 4AW. Tel: 0345 777 3322 email: information@ecclesiastical.com

Ecclesiastical Law Society https://ecclawsoc.org.uk *Executive Secretary,* The Rt Revd J. F. Ford, 1 The Sanctuary, London, SW1P 3JT. email: admin@ecclawsoc.org.uk and via website

English Clergy Association, The https://www.clergyassoc.co.uk *Chairman*, The Revd C. Messervy, LLM, BTh, The Rectory, 12 Cricketers Way, Haddenham, HP17 8FL email: cassamesservy@gmail.com

Feed the Minds www.feedtheminds.org *CEO*, L. Moore (*Interim*), The Foundry, 17 Oval Way, London, SE11 5RR. Tel: 020 3752 5797 email: info@feedtheminds.org

Fellowship of Contemplative Prayer, The www.contemplative-prayer.org.uk *Chair*, The Revd J. C. Hill email: admin@contemplative-prayer.org.uk

Fellowship of St Alban and St Sergius https://fsass.org *General Secretary*, Rev. C. K. W. Moore, 1 Canterbury Road, Oxford, OX2 6LU. Tel: 01865 552 991 email: gensec@sobornost.org

Forward in Faith https://forwardinfaith.com *Director,* T. Middleton, St Andrew Holborn, 5 St Andrew Street, London, EC4A 3AF. Tel: 07368 124811 email: director@forwardinfaith.com

Girls Friendly Society https://girlsfriendlysociety.org.uk *Chief Executive Officer*, H. Smith, 3rd Floor, 86–90 Paul Street, London, EC2A 4NE. Tel: 020 7837 9669 email: info@girlsfriendlysociety.org.uk

Girlguiding https://www.girlguiding.org.uk *Chief Executive*, A. Salt, 17–19 Buckingham Palace Road, London, SW1W 0PT. Tel: 0800 999 2016 email: via website

Girls' Brigade Ministries https://www.girlsbrigadeministries.org.uk *CEO*, Judith Davey-Cole, Cliff College, Calver, Hope Valley, Derbyshire, S32 3XG. Tel: 01246 582322 email: judith.davey@gb-ministries.org

Guild of All Souls, The https://www.guildofallsouls.org.uk *General Secretary*, V. Cole, Dalton House, 60 Windsor Avenue, London, SW19 2RR. Tel: 07498 778691 email: guildofallsouls@outlook.com and via website

Guild of Church Musicians, The https://gcm.org.uk *President*, Dame M. Archer, 3 Sewards End, Wickford, Essex, SS12 9PB. email: via website

Guild of Health and St Raphael, The https://gohealth.org.uk *Chief Executive Officer*, The Revd Dr G. Straine, 2nd Floor, Regis House, 45 King William Street, London, EC4R 9AN. email: via website

Guild of Servants of the Sanctuary https://guildofservantsofthesanctuary.co.uk *Secretary General*, M. Andrew, c/o ACS, 16 Commercial Street, Birmingham, B1 1RS. email: gss.secretarygeneral@gmail.com and via website

Guild of Vergers, The Church of England https://cofegv.org.uk *General Secretary,* S. Stokes, 124 City Road, London, EC1V 2NX. email: CEGVGenSec@gmail.com

Hymn Society of Great Britain and Ireland, The https://hymnsocietygbi.org.uk *Secretary,* The Revd R. A. Canham, Windrush, Braithwaite, Keswick, CA12 5SZ. Tel: 0176 877 8054 email: via website

Intercontinental Church Society https://www.ics-uk.org *Mission Director*, R. Bromley, Unit 11, Ensign Business Centre, Westwood Way, Westwood Business Park, Coventry, CV4 8JA. email: via website

Jerusalem and Middle East Church Association https://www.jmeca.org.uk *Secretary*, S. Eason, 1 Hart House, The Hart, Farnham, Surrey, GU9 7HJ. Tel: 01252 726994 email: information@jmeca.org.uk

Keston Institute https://www.keston.org.uk *Chair,* X. Dennen, 47 South Street, Durham, DH1 4QP. email: administrator@keston.org.uk and via website

Leprosy Mission, The https://www.leprosymission.org.uk *Chief Executive Officer,* P. Waddup, Goldhay Way, Orton Goldhay, Peterborough, PE2 5GZ. Tel: 01733 370505 email: via website

Lesbian and Gay Christian Movement https://www.onebodyonefaith.org.uk *Executive Director,* L. Dowding. Tel: 01636 673072 email: via website

Methodist Church, The https://www.methodist.org.uk *Secretary of the Conference,* The Revd Dr J. Hustler, Methodist Church House, 25 Tavistock Place, London, WC1H 9SF. Tel: 020 7467 3794 email: soc@methodistchurch.org.uk

Mission to Seafarers, The https://www.missiontoseafarers.org *Secretary General*, P. Rouch, 1st floor, 6 Bath Place, Rivington Street, London, EC2A 3JE. Tel: 020 7248 5202 email: via website

Modern Church www.modernchurch.org.uk *General Secretary*, A. Webster, Modern Church, 22 The Kiln, Burgess Hill, West Sussex, RH15 0LU. Tel: 0845 345 1909 email: Gensec@modernchurch.org.uk and via website

Moravian Church British Province, The www.moravian.org.uk *Administrator*, L. Newens, Moravian Church House, 5 Muswell Hill, London, N10 3TJ. Tel: 020 8883 3409 email: office@moravian.org.uk and via website

Mothers' Union https://www.mothersunion.org *Chief Executive,* B. Jullien, Mary Sumner House, 24 Tufton Street, London, SW1P 3RB. Tel: 020 7222 5533 email: via website

National Churches Trust www.nationalchurchestrust.org *Chief Executive,* C. Walker, 7 Tufton Street, London, SW1P 3QB. Tel: 020 7222 0605 email: info@nationalchurchestrust.org and via website

Open Synod Group https://opensynodgroup.org *Chair*, P. Allen. email: mrspennyallen@yahoo.co.uk

Orthodox Church http://www.sgois.co.uk St George Orthodox Information Service, The White House, Mettingham, NR35 1TP. Tel: 01986 895176 email: stgeorgeois@aol.com and via website

Partnership for World Mission https://www.churchofengland.org/resources/world-mission Church House, Great Smith Street, London, SW1P 3AZ. Tel: 020 7898 1000 email: via website

Prayer Book Society, The https://www.pbs.org.uk *Company Secretary*, B. F. Smith, The Studio, Copyhold Farm, Lady Grove, Goring Heath, Reading, RG8 7RT. Tel: 0118 984 2582 email: pbs.admin@pbs.org.uk

Prison Fellowship https://prisonfellowship.org.uk *Chief Executive Officer*, C. De Souza, PO Box 68226, London, SW1P 9WR. Tel: 020 7799 2500 email: info@prisonfellowship.org.uk and via website

Quakers in Britain https://www.quaker.org.uk Friends House, 173 Euston Road, London, NW1 2BJ. Tel: 020 7663 1000 email: enquiries@quaker.org.uk

Radius (The Religious Drama Society of Great Britain) https://www.radiusdrama.org.uk 4 Carpenter Avenue, Llandudno, LL30 1YW. email: info@radius.org.uk and via website

Retreat Association, The www.retreats.org.uk *Director*, A. MacTier, PO Box 1130, Princes Risborough, Buckinghamshire, HP22 9RP. Tel: 01494 569 056 email: info@retreats.org.uk and via website

Royal School of Church Music, The https://www.rscm.org.uk *Director*, H. Morris, 19 The Close, Salisbury, Wiltshire, SP1 2EB. Tel: 01722 424848 email: enquiries@rscm.com and via website

Rural Theology Association, The https://ruraltheologyassociation.com *Secretary*, The Revd A. Stevenson email: via website

St Luke's for Clergy Wellbeing https://www.stlukesforclergy.org.uk *Chief Executive*, Dr C. Walker, Room 201, Church House, Great Smith Street, London, SW1P 3AZ. Tel: 020 4546 7000 email: enquiries@stlukesforclergy.org.uk and via website

St Marylebone Healing and Counselling Centre https://marylebone-hcc.org.uk *Director of Clinical Services*, S. Hyde, 17 Marylebone Road, London, NW1 5LT. Tel: 020 7935 5066 email: hcc@stmarylebone.org

Salvation Army, The https://www.salvationarmy.org.uk *Commissioners*, P. and J. Main, Territorial Headquarters, 1 Champion Park, London, SE5 8FJ Tel: 020 7367 4500 email: info@salvationarmy.org.uk

Scout Association, The https://www.scouts.org.uk *Chief Executive*, A. Jones, Gilwell Park, Chingford, London, E4 7QW. Information Centre: 0345 300 1818 email: info.centre@scouts.org.uk

Scripture Union https://scriptureunion.org.uk *National Director*, D. Newton, Trinity House, Opal Court, Opal Drive, Fox Milne, Milton Keynes, MK15 0DF. Tel: 01908 856000 email: hello@scriptureunion.org.uk and via website

Society for Promoting Christian Knowledge, The *See page 307.*

Student Christian Movement https://www.movement.org.uk *Chief Executive Officer*, The Revd N. Nixon, Grays Court, 3 Nursery Road, Edgbaston, Birmingham, B15 3JX. Tel: 0121 426 4918 email: scm@movement.org.uk

Theatre Chaplaincy UK https://theatrechaplaincyuk.com *Senior Chaplain*, The Revd L. Meader, St Paul's Church, Bedford Street, London, WC2E 9ED. Tel: 07501 829491 email: info@theatrechaplaincyuk.com

Theology (the journal) https://journals.sagepub.com/home/TJX *Editor*, R. Gill, Sage Publications Ltd, 1 Oliver's Yard, 55 City Road, London, EC1Y 1SP. Tel: 020 7324 8500 email: theology@spck.org.uk

Toc H https://www.toch-uk.org.uk *Chief Executive Officer*, P. Hackwood, 483 Green Lanes, London, N13 4BS. Tel: 020 8057 4200 email: info@toch.org.uk

UCCF: The Christian Unions https://www.uccf.org.uk *CEO*, Matt Lillicrap, Blue Boar House, 5 Blue Boar Street, Oxford, OX1 4EE. Tel: 01865 253678 email: info@uccf.org.uk

United Reformed Church, The https://urc.org.uk *General Secretary,* The Revd Dr J. Bradbury, United Reformed Church House, 86 Tavistock Place, London, WC1H 9RT. Tel: 020 7916 2020 email: urc@urc.org.uk and via website

USPG https://uspg.org.uk *General Secretary,* Revd Dr D. Dormor, 5 Trinity Street, London, SE1 1DB. Tel: 020 7921 2200 email: info@uspg.org.uk

WATCH (Women and the Church) https://www.womenandthechurch.org *Chair,* Revd M. Oborne, 14 Ashford Close, Fordingbridge, Hampshire, SP6 1DH. email: admin@womenandthechurch.org

Week of Prayer for World Peace https://weekofprayerforworldpeace.co.uk c/o 112 Whittlesey Road, March, PE15 0AH. email: wpwp2021@yahoo.com

World Day of Prayer https://www.wwdp.org.uk *Administrator,* V. Daniell, Commercial Road, Tunbridge Wells, Kent, TN1 2RR. Tel: 01892 541411 email: office@wwdp.org.uk

YMCA https://ymca.org.uk *Chief Executive Officer and National Secretary*, D. Hatton, YMCA England and Wales, 10–11 Charterhouse Square, London, EC1M 6EH. Tel: 020 7186 9500 email: enquiries@ymca.org.uk

Young Women's Trust https://www.youngwomenstrust.org *Chief Executive*, C. Reindorp, Unit 1.01 Wenlock Studios, 50–52 Wharf Road, London, N1 7EU. Tel: 020 7837 2019 email: info@youngwomenstrust.org and via website

The Society for Promoting Christian Knowledge

Founded in 1698.

36 Causton Street, London, SW1P 4ST

Telephone: 020 7592 3900 email: spck@spck.org.uk and via website

website: https://spckpublishing.co.uk

SPCK is the Anglican mission agency working through publishing. Our vision is creating conversations between Christianity and culture. Our mission is publishing great Christian books around the world. We are committed to sharing innovative Christian thinking to enable people of all backgrounds to increase their understanding of the Christian faith. SPCK publishes under a range of imprints, including SPCK, Marylebone House, Form, Inter-Varsity Press, Apollos, Lion, Candle and York Courses. Each year, we sell half a million books and apps; our books have been translated into more than 100 languages; we have 50,000 web visitors every month. Profits from sales of these books are used to support our programmes, such as the free Assemblies website (https://www.Assemblies.org.uk), the free Home Groups website (https://HomeGroups.org.uk), the African Theological Network Press and Diffusion Prison Fiction. We also work with Clergy Support Trust to make available the Clergy Support Trust library, containing more than a thousand e-books which are free to all ordinands and curates.

Memoranda

Memoranda

Memoranda

Memoranda

Memoranda

Addresses

Name

Address

Telephone

Mobile

Email

Name

Address

Telephone

Mobile

Email

Name

Address

Telephone

Mobile

Email

Addresses

Name

Address

Telephone

Mobile

Email

Name

Address

Telephone

Mobile

Email

Name

Address

Telephone

Mobile

Email

Addresses

Name

Address

Telephone

Mobile

Email

Name

Address

Telephone

Mobile

Email

Name

Address

Telephone

Mobile

Email

Addresses

Name

Address

Telephone

Mobile

Email

Name

Address

Telephone

Mobile

Email

Name

Address

Telephone

Mobile

Email

Addresses

Name

Address

Telephone

Mobile

Email

Name

Address

Telephone

Mobile

Email

Name

Address

Telephone

Mobile

Email

Addresses

Name

Address

Telephone

Mobile

Email

Name

Address

Telephone

Mobile

Email

Name

Address

Telephone

Mobile

Email

Addresses

Name

Address

Telephone

Mobile

Email

Name

Address

Telephone

Mobile

Email

Name

Address

Telephone

Mobile

Email

Addresses

Name

Address

Telephone

Mobile

Email

Name

Address

Telephone

Mobile

Email

Name

Address

Telephone

Mobile

Email

Addresses

Name

Address

Telephone

Mobile

Email

Name

Address

Telephone

Mobile

Email

Name

Address

Telephone

Mobile

Email